C·H·A·I·N
REACTION

C·H·A·I·N
REACTION

D. James Kennedy
T.M. Moore

WORD PUBLISHING
Word (UK) Ltd
England
WORD BOOKS AUSTRALIA
Heathmont, Victoria, Australia
SUNDAY SCHOOL CENTRE WHOLESALE
Salt River, South Africa
ALBY COMMERCIAL ENTERPRISES PTE LTD
Scotts Road, Singapore 0922
CHRISTIAN MARKETING LTD
Auckland, New Zealand

CHAIN REACTION!

ISBN 0-85009-077-6

Scripture quotations are from the Authorised King James Version of
the Bible.

Reproduced, printed and bound in Great Britain by Hazell, Watson
and Viney Limited, Member of the BPCC Group, Aylesbury, Bucks.

To
the generation of world changers
even now arising in our midst

Contents

Introduction

All around us an emerging ground swell of people yearns and clamors for change. Our generation has struggled with forces of oppression, against powers and tides of immorality and godlessness, and through wastelands of economic disillusionment. The people of our society are weary with the life they have made for themselves, and they long for something better and more permanent.

There are, moreover, new voices being heard, promising the change and deliverance that the people of this age so earnestly desire. Marxism woos the millions of the Third World with a deception so powerful that it can scarcely be resisted. New theories of economics and government promise unprecedented peace and prosperity for the free nations of the West. The mystery and allure of the information age have attracted the attention of nearly everyone and promise the moon, the stars, and a virtually unlimited future for mankind.

All these voices and more besides offer the men and women of this age a vision of the change they so earnestly desire. Yet none of them can fully deliver, for none of them is anchored to the unshakeable Rock of God's revealed Word. Only a program of change—a blueprint for revolution—that stands squarely and broadly on this inspired and eternal foundation will be able to satisfy the longing and needs of this or any generation.

In this book we have attempted to set forth the broad outlines of a direction for change which can be charted only from within the evangelical Christian community. We do not pretend to have exhausted the scope of so challenging an endeavor as our present situation requires. Rather, we have sought mainly to stimulate the interest of evangelical believers for a broader, more powerful and effective Christian faith than they have ever known before. We hope to rekindle the flame of evangelism that has flickered low in recent years. We want to generate interest in new fields and new directions of application for the eternal truths of the gospel. And, above all, we want to convince readers that they can make a difference, that they can be used of God to help take the first steps in a broad-based Christian revolution, which can change the social, cultural, and moral topography of our nation for generations to come.

The book touches on what we consider to be the fundamental areas of change in which every believer can begin to assert a dynamic Christian presence. Based first of all on the belief that each of us must commit to a more vital and involved Christian faith, the book moves on to a consideration of the primary place of the Bible and of evangelism as the cornerstone and foundation of the Christian moral and social edifice. It then moves on to demonstrate the guarantee of success that the finished work of Christ holds forth and calls the reader to more effective and concentrated Christian living in the home, in personal stewardship, in political responsibilities, in the work of education, and on the job. Finally, the book summons us all to a more comprehensive and powerful life of prayer and concentration on Jesus as the quintessential World Changer for us to follow.

Study questions and additional suggestions for reading follow each chapter. These can be used for individual study or group discussion. Since much of the material for this book derives from our own experience in ministry and in our personal walks with the Lord, we have not sought entirely to eliminate the use of the first-person-singular pronoun. In some instances it will be obvious which of us is guiding the discussion. In the others it will be irrelevant. Together we have committed ourselves to the precepts and convictions set forth in each chapter.

We send out this book in the hope and with the prayer that it will challenge your faith and excite you with a new vision of what we might be able to achieve for the greater glory of God. There is a world to be changed, and we are the people to change it. Here's to the world changers of this generation!

Fort Lauderdale, Florida   D. James Kennedy
Summer 1985   T. M. Moore

1

For Such a Time As This

"They Changed the World"

Only once in a great while does there arise a generation of men and women of whom it can be said, "They changed the world." Only rarely in the flow of human history does there come about just the right combination of circumstances, attitudes, opportunities, and actions that serves to launch the course of history in an altogether different direction. Numerous examples could be cited.

Those 120 men and women, praying together in an upper room (Acts, chapters 1 and 2) found themselves in the midst of just such a situation. Their courage, persistence, and faith began a movement of God's grace that within just a few short years "turned the world upside down" (Acts 17:6).

Saint Augustine, bishop of the North African city of Hippo, could not have known, as he penned in A.D. 425 the final words to his *City of God,* that history had prepared him and his followers to rescue the stability of Western culture for over a thousand years, through the ideas presented in that volume.

Martin Luther and John Calvin, in the sixteenth century, could not possibly have foreseen that their courageous efforts to revitalize European civilization would lead to the liberties and blessings that free men and women everywhere enjoy and hold dear today.

Nor could John and Charles Wesley have known that their preaching and teaching among the downcast and the working classes would spare England from the blood and violence of the French Revolution.

Our Puritan forefathers, who in faith braved the storms of the Atlantic and the uncertainties of an uncharted world, could not possibly have foreseen what their courageous actions would lead to in just a few short generations. Nor could John Witherspoon, John Adams, Patrick Henry, and those others whose Christian faith led them to resist political oppression and the subversion of their liberties foretell that the new nation they were creating would become the greatest that history had ever known.

And what shall we say of such as Aleksandr Solzhenitsyn, Mother Teresa, or Francis Schaeffer? Time has yet to tell how their courage, compassion, and faith will contribute to shaping the flow of history in some new and vastly more exciting way.

And there are many others, less well known, whose faith, at just the right time and in just the right manner, led them to believe God in the midst of great challenges and difficult tasks. Their persistence in following the leading of God enabled them to impact the flow of history in a significant and enduring manner. They are the world changers, the people who truly made a difference by affecting the events of their day and shaping the course of history.

But the real question before us is "What about you and me?" Ours is a day that cries out for a new generation of world changers. Will it be said of us that in this generation we were a people who seized the moment and poured ourselves out to change the world? Is it possible that God may be presenting us with the challenge of changing the world in our time? Or will we simply become another of the countless generations of men and women who made no significant change in the prevailing tide?

Will we be numbered among those who have truly changed the world?

Rather, let us put it this way: We *will* change the world. This generation of Christians, by their action or inaction, will make the determinative choices as to the unfolding of history in the years immediately ahead. We will either consciously, aggressively, and persistently labor to mold things after the pattern of

God's truth—or we will, by our neglect, see them fashioned according to an altogether different standard.

We believe God wants us to change the world. We believe He wants this world to begin to reflect His beauty, His holiness, His truth, and His love. We believe God is weary with the sin and sorrow of mankind, and we believe He is determined to do an altogether new and exciting work in shaping the flow of history today. We believe He is raising up a generation of men and women who will take Him at His Word and, with careful forethought and unparalleled courage and conviction, undertake the effort necessary to change the world.

These people will be the world changers of our day, and we believe God is preparing them right now for such a time as this.

But how can we know this? And how can each one of us make certain that he or she is found among the world changers of this generation?

We can begin to find some answers to these questions by looking to the example of one of the great world changers of the Old Testament.

A Reluctant World Changer

Queen Esther had been placed on the throne of Persia at the demise of the rebellious Vashti, deposed queen of mighty Ahasuerus. In the course of time a plot against the Jews was devised. The plot was designed to destroy them as a people, and it came to the attention of Mordecai, Esther's stepfather. He rightly perceived that immediate widespread action was required by Jews throughout the Persian Empire and that Esther was the one properly positioned to initiate it. In Esther 4:1–16 we read the following:

1 When Mordecai perceived all that was done, Mordecai rent his clothes, and put on sackcloth with ashes, and went out into the midst of the city, and cried with a loud and bitter cry;
2 And came even before the king's gate: for none might enter into the king's gate clothed with sackcloth.
3 And in every province, whithersoever the king's commandment and his decree came, there was great mourning among the Jews, and fasting, and weeping, and wailing; and many lay in sackcloth and ashes.

4 So Esther's maids and her chamberlains came and told it to her. Then was the queen exceedingly grieved; and she sent raiment to clothe Mordecai, and to take away his sackcloth from him: but he received it not.

5 Then called Esther for Hatach, one of the king's chamberlains, whom he had appointed to attend upon her, and gave him a commandment to Mordecai, to know what it was, and why it was.

6 So Hatach went forth to Mordecai unto the street of the city, which was before the king's gate.

7 And Mordecai told him of all that had happened unto him, and of the sum of the money that Haman had promised to pay to the king's treasuries for the Jews, to destroy them.

8 Also he gave him the copy of the writing of the decree that was given at Shushan to destroy them, to shew it unto Esther, and to declare it unto her, and to charge her that she should go in unto the king, to make supplication unto him, and to make request before him for her people.

9 And Hatach came and told Esther the words of Mordecai.

10 Again Esther spake unto Hatach, and gave him comandment unto Mordecai;

11 All the king's servants, and the people of the king's provinces, do know, that whosoever, whether man or woman, shall come unto the king into the inner court, who is not called, there is one law of his to put him to death, except such to whom the king shall hold out the golden sceptre, that he may live: but I have not been called to come in unto the king these thirty days.

12 And they told to Mordecai Esther's words.

13 Then Mordecai commanded to answer Esther, Think not with thyself that thou shalt escape in the king's house, more than all the Jews.

14 For if thou altogether holdest thy peace at this time, then shall there enlargement and deliverance arise to the Jews from another place; but thou and thy father's house shall be destroyed: and who knoweth whether thou art come to the kingdom for such a time as this?

15 Then Esther bade them return Mordecai this answer,

16 Go, gather together all the Jews that are present in Shushan, and fast ye for me, and neither eat nor drink three days, night or day: I also and my maidens will fast likewise; and so will I go in unto the king, which is not according to the law: and if I perish, I perish.

Now let us observe some specifics from this passage. Mordecai knew that the situation facing the Jews was extremely critical. The machinery had been set in motion to destroy the Jews in Persia. They had to mobilize to preserve their lives and liberties. Something had to be done, and it had to begin somewhere. Thus, Mordecai sent Hatach back to Queen Esther "to charge her that she should go in unto the king, to make supplication unto him, and to make request before him for her people" (v. 8). These were specific actions devised by Mordecai, prescribed for the one whom he perceived to be most favorably positioned to change the course of history. Mordecai knew Esther's faithful action would create a situation that would enable others to act as well.

Notice, however, that Esther immediately responded by pointing out the obstacles to her taking the specific action presented (v. 11). It was almost certain that she would meet death— at the very least, we might suppose, a beating or a severe and humiliating rebuke—for approaching the Persian monarch uninvited. How could she be expected to act when her own peace would be jeopardized? Thus, she sent word to Mordecai that for the sake of her own personal well-being, she could not take the necessary action.

Mordecai is quick to show her, however, that her failure to act at that moment would redound to the destruction of her well-being, her freedom, and her very life (v. 13). The risks of inaction were vastly more fearful than those of action. Esther could either act in faith and make an effort to change history, or receive from history the blows that her inaction would bring. Mordecai wanted her to see that the status quo was but a temporary situation; history was changing rapidly, and she would, one way or another, by her acting or failing to act, make a difference in the direction it took.

Thus, he charged her to act, to believe that by her action she could be a means of helping to guarantee the freedoms and blessings the people of God had come to know (v. 14). Although she could not be certain, Esther must believe that God had put her in this place, at this time, under these circumstances, in order to change the world. She could sit back no longer. She had to become involved, regardless of the risk or cost: "And who knoweth whether thou art come to the kingdom for such a time as this?"

"For Such a Time As This"

"For such a time as this." Esther's courage and resourcefulness saved her people. Her willingness to risk her personal comfort and her well-being in a bold and challenging scheme was taken by God as the spark to ignite a systematic and comprehensive effort among the Jews in Persia to guarantee their liberties into the future. Her action enabled and encouraged tens of thousands of others to do what had to be done to prevent disaster.

The conditions of the day required action. Religious and personal liberties were at stake. Key people such as Mordecai and Esther were strategically placed to be able to make a difference. Untold scores of thousands were scattered about the kingdom, ready to do their part in making certain that the freedoms of their present were guaranteed into the future. And they all, like one great body in orchestrated movement together, acted in the belief that they could make a difference. They could change their world, convinced that even their smallest efforts would make a difference. It was their faithfulness, their courage, and their determined effort that God honored to guarantee the freedom of His people for the generations to come.

"For such a time *is* this." We have come in our day to a point in history not unlike that which Mordecai faced in his. All around us are those who, in the name of personal rights or governmental prerogatives, would take away the freedoms of Christian men and women to worship and serve God as they choose.

Already they are determined to shut down our Christian schools. The engines of government and the courts are even today gearing up to control or destroy the education of children in the classrooms of Christian schools and in Christian homes all over America.

Subtle encroachments on our right to worship are also being tested. Even now there are sections of America where home Bible studies are being declared unlawful because they "transgress the rights of neighbors."

Courts are acting to interfere with the preaching of the Word of God in public. The Bible and prayer have been effectively banished from those very public-school classrooms that two hundred years ago literally depended on these activities to stabilize the entire process of instruction.

Traditional holidays commemorating significant events in the Christian calendar are mocked and modified by law, reduced to a shadow of their true significance.

Canons of morality repugnant to Christians for generations are being protected by law and supported and encouraged even from within the household of the faith. Homosexuality, divorce, adultery, and other immoral practices, which have historically undermined the very fabric of society, are today being protected by a framework of law. One day they will turn on that very law and destroy it.

The media of the land, traditionally the responsible source of information and understanding, are today the conduits of distortion, immorality, and anti-Christian bias, poisoning the minds of Americans before the light of truth can shine there with all its brilliance.

Enterprises of Christian compassion are threatened with being taxed or zoned out of existence. Christian parents are threatened with having their children educated by godless mentors. The sanctity of life is destroyed by courts and medical practitioners whose hands are red with the blood of millions of slaughtered innocents. And, internationally, our government continues to seek ways of placating and appeasing a Marxist government that every day for all the years of its existence has labored to crush our brothers and sisters in Christ under the heel of atheistic militarism.

The circumstances and conditions of our day shout aloud that the destruction of Christian freedoms is descending upon us with a fury. While we refuse to risk action for the sake of our present comfort, we must remind ourselves that as the course of history changes to destroy the freedoms we hold dear today, those changes will indiscriminately and with a vengeance break upon each one of us and bring to an end our world as we know it. Truly, we will change history in our day. The only question is "In what way?"

For such a time as this. Indeed.

But we believe that God has so prepared the totality of the present historical scenario that a generation of modern world changers, committed to persistent action in His name, could make for an altogether different future. We believe that the circumstances of our land are such that if we will act now, act often, and act together, we can not only preserve our freedoms but extend the blessings of God's grace into the future for years to come. If we will commit ourselves to becoming world changers in our day, we can make a difference in the course of history. We can change our world in a direction more consistent with that which is prescribed in the Word of God.

The Opportunity and the Challenge

Much that is happening in America today should convince us that our individual actions in the name of Christian freedom can make a difference. There are today nearly forty-five million men and women in this nation who describe themselves as "intensely religious."[1]

That is, more than one out of every five Americans believes that God loves them, and claims they actively engage in prayer, attend religious services, read the Bible, encourage others to turn to religion, and listen to religious broadcasts. Those forty-five million people constitute a vast potential for righteousness, truth, and love. If those millions had a committed corps of world changers to follow into action, what might be accomplished?

These forty-five million people are described as "likely to vote often and to become highly involved in their local communities." If they only had an army of committed world changers enlightening their voting and guiding their community involvement, this great mass could provide a force for righteousness and truth against which not even the gates of hell could prevail!

Furthermore, what kind of impact could this great body of people, led by those who are consciously committed to changing the world, have on the 75 percent of all Americans who describe themselves as religious and as open to becoming even more involved in religious matters?[2] Indeed, as Jesus said, the fields "are white already to harvest" (John 4:35)—if only we can enlist the harvesters and a corps of world changers to lead and train them.

Efforts are already under way to motivate and train those millions so that we can commission the vast majority of all Americans in the cause of Jesus Christ and Christian freedom. Yet, there is still lacking a clearly defined nucleus for the effort. There is yet to be developed a corps of like-minded, action-oriented men and women who will follow the Lord's guidance into the leadership responsibilities that this great effort will require. To motivate the forty-five million "intensely religious" Americans, so as to be able to sway 75 percent of all Americans to change the course of history, will take a million—one million—world changers. These will be people who, like Mordecai, perceive the danger before us. They will be people like Esther who take the risks despite the obstacles or dangers. They will be people like those unnamed and unnumbered Jews in the Persian Empire who worked together to protect their liberties and preserve their world. They will know that even their smallest act of faith is meaningful toward the goal of changing the flow of history. They will believe God has called them to lead for such a time as this, so that our world can be truly changed!

They will be people like you and me.

What can we expect these world changers to accomplish? In the first place, we might expect that they could tip the balance back in favor of the traditional family. Despite any threats to its survival, George Gallup has observed that "the American public is voting in favor of the classic traditional family—in their future hopes as well as in their near past history. The vast majority of North Americans see the family as the cornerstone of society and the best hope for a positive future."[3]

It might be that a coterie of world changers, sufficiently motivated and equipped, could lead the way to greater stability in the homes of America. Through their example and their actions of faith, love, and help, they could be used to save marriages and restore lost children to their parents. By reaching out in love to encourage and assist in creative and effective ways, one million world changers leading millions of their fellow believers in specific actions of love and concern could return our society to its family-centered basis in a very short time.

How about the schools? Could one million world changers make a difference in the quality of American education? Already we have examples of Christians who have worked effectively to make changes in the types of textbooks that are used in public schools. Could one million world changers make even more significant contributions in this area? Further, there is a growing number of Christian parents involved in the home-school movement, parents who are becoming increasingly involved in fulfilling their biblical mandate to be the responsible agents in the education of their children. Likewise, the Christian day-school movement continues to grow and prosper, with new schools being added to the existing hundreds each day. There are Christian textbooks, Christian films, Christian curricula, Christian school associations, and even Christian graduate schools providing Christian teachers for the children of the land.

Could one million world changers help to further the cause of Christian education? By meeting with public-school leaders, serving on school boards, protesting ungodliness in schools, and assisting Christian parents and teachers in a myriad of ways, what kind of lasting impression could one million world changers make? They could create an enormous impact, indeed.

What kind of influence could one million world changers exert over the decisions reached in the various lawmaking bodies of our nation? How could these committed men and women help to return the moral fiber of America to a more biblical base, through their efforts in voting and working for godly statutes? One million active world changers could certainly be used of God to reach and motivate vast numbers of people to work for a legal framework in America that clearly distinguishes between morality and immorality, truth and lies, decency and obscenity. They could help to create an altogether different atmosphere in the nation in just a short while.

And for what else might we dare to hope? Can we envision the end of abortion? Could a million world changers help to bring that about? Is it possible that we might see churches revitalized to become the total community service centers they once were? Can we help to bring more responsibility back to the media? Could we activate the Christian media to become a more significant force in America? Can new meaning be brought to the workplace? Could unemployment, inflation, and other economic woes be addressed and genuinely effective solutions implemented? Can human relationships be reinforced to take on new meaning? Can effective help and encouragement be brought to imprisoned believers in Communist lands? Can millions and millions of Americans be brought to a saving knowledge of our Lord Jesus Christ?

We believe it can be done. We are told that "the impact of religious belief reaches far beyond the realm of politics, and has penetrated virtually every dimension of American experience. This force is rapidly becoming a more powerful factor in American life than whether someone is liberal or conservative, male or female, young or old, or a blue-collar or white-collar worker."[4] That incalculable power, that sleeping giant, is ready to be roused into action for the cause of Jesus Christ and His righteousness. This great potential lacks only the corps of faithful world changers to motivate and lead it into action.

We believe that as a people we can be part of the vast army of world changers who will make the difference in American history over the next few years. No obstacle is too great, no want is beyond supply, no task is beyond our doing—if only we can believe strongly enough that God will use our every step of faith, regardless how small, to change our world and preserve our Christian freedoms. There are one million world changers being called out for action right now. We must resolve to be among them.

But what will it take? What will be required on our part?

A Call to Productive Faith

Essentially, what is required is something that many of us already possess as a gift from God—faith. Jesus said that nothing would be impossible to us if only we had faith that God would accomplish our designs for His glory (Matt. 17:20). Certainly God "is able to do exceeding abundantly above all that we ask or think" (Eph. 3:20). Nothing, absolutely nothing that we might hope to achieve for His glory will be impossible for God (Luke 18:27). All that remains to be seen is whether or not we can believe God will do it through us.

To change the world as God would have it changed will require faith on our part, but faith of a particular kind. Hebrews 11 tells us about that faith.

We recognize Hebrews 11 as being the great chapter on "heroes of the faith," men and women who stood firm for the faith against the greatest obstacles. We generally tend to see this chapter as emphasizing the importance of a professing faith, one that refuses to deny God regardless of the difficulty or suffering that may ensue. And certainly today we need, every one of us, to be sure that we have a professing faith. We must be ready to preach the gospel to every creature in every season. We must stand courageously against the threats and mockings of a hostile world and hold forth the truth of the gospel regardless of the cost to us personally.

But there is another dimension of faith discussed in this chapter. This we might call productive faith, a faith that—because it recognizes specific needs and envisions long-range results—is impelled into action toward the achievement of those results, no matter what the cost. It is a faith that produces tangible results within the flow of history, a faith that changes the world. This productive faith is mentioned in Hebrews 11:33-34:"Who through faith subdued kingdoms, wrought righteousness, obtained promises, stopped the mouths of lions, Quenched the violence of fire, escaped the edge of the sword, out of weakness were made strong, waxed valiant in fight, turned to flight the armies of the aliens."

Here are clear examples of heroes of the faith who literally changed the world. They subdued kingdoms, instilling the reign of God in place of the godlessness and immorality of heathen religions. They took whatever steps of faith were necessary to root out sin and wickedness and establish godliness in the land. They wrought righteousness, banishing evil by the sheer force of their presence. They obtained promises, securing from God the realization in their day of the things He had committed Himself to do through them. They changed the world because they believed that God would honor even their smallest steps of faith, their most isolated actions toward the goals they had in mind.

These heroes had a faith in God that moved them to action for His name's sake. And, in their time, they made the difference between godlessness and righteousness, evil and goodness.

We need today to couple our professing faith with a resolute and powerful productive faith. We need, that is, to commit ourselves to a vocal faith as well as to strategic, determined, persistent, and coordinated actions toward the long-range goal of changing the world.

Failing to believe that we can do this is to cast aspersions on the integrity and faithfulness of our God. It is to deny His claim to being the same yesterday, today, and forever, the Lord God who changes not. For He has, through generations of world changers in the past, done exactly the kinds of things that must be done today. He has raised up world changers who have made an impact for Him through the power of His Spirit and Word. And God's power and determination to see this world reflect His glory is not diminished in our time. He stands ready to change the world.

And we believe that this generation—you and I and all our brothers and sisters in Christ—have been put here in this moment of history for such a time as this. To us is the challenge—and the opportunity—to be the world changers of our day.

Granted, the odds are against us. As Jeremy Rifkin notes:

> . . . many middle-class Christians are falling back more and more on the old notion of the "gospel of wealth," equating biblical doctrine with rugged individualism, free enterprise, and unlimited material accumulation. This kind of expansionist theology is still very much a dominant motif in American Christianity. The "gospel of wealth" theme will likely continue to be used by individual Christians to justify a lack of concern or involvement with the pressing economic needs ahead. . . . For these Christians, the evangelical movement will serve as a sanctuary for withdrawal from the turmoil around them.[5]

These will not be the world changers for our time. Our day requires faithful men and women, one million strong, who believe that God will use them to change the world. They will develop an entirely new outlook on life. They will begin to see every problem in our society as an affront to the glory of God, a challenge to the world changers of our day, and an opportunity for productive faith to be put to work. They will plan regularly the steps of productive faith that they must take in order to make an impact for the gospel of Jesus Christ. They will see His cross as the central event of history, His gospel as the central truth for all men, and His cause as the only thing ultimately worth living for. They will work individually and in groups. They will make phone calls, write letters, distribute literature, picket, protest, preach, and undertake a score of seemingly insignificant tasks that when taken together and faithfully performed week in and week out will have an impact for righteousness that cannot be calculated at this time!

They will, we believe, change the world. For they will see that God, who has given them new life in Jesus Christ, is determined to use them to spread that new life and all its benefits to others in our land by all means and in all seasons. They will commit themselves to this at all costs, and they are being raised up, at this very moment, for the opportunities and challenges before us in these days.

We must make certain that we are part of this corps of world changers. We must determine to seek ways of becoming informed about the needs of our day and of sharing those needs with others. We must prepare ourselves to take specific actions that will assert the truth of God and manifest His presence in every need with which we are faced. We must refuse to believe that any action is too small, any strategy too unreachable. We must determine to call others to faith in Jesus Christ and to exemplify His love and truth in our everyday lives. We must pray, plan, preach, and persevere. We must, in other words, determine that we will be the generation, we who name the name of Jesus Christ, that charts the course for history in the coming months and years.

"And who knoweth whether thou art come to the kingdom for such a time as this?"

Notes

1. Connecticut Mutual Insurance Co., *The Connecticut Mutual Life Report on American Values in the '80's: The Impact of Belief* (Hartford, Conn., 1981), pp. 17–30.

2. Ibid.

3. George Gallup, Jr. and David Poling, *The Search for America's Faith* (Nashville: Abingdon, 1980).

4. Connecticut Mutual, p. 6.

5. Jeremy Rifkin with Ted Howard, *Entropy* (New York: The Viking Press, 1980), p. 240.

Questions for Study or Discussion

1. In Esther's case, what would have been the likely consequences of her not becoming involved?

2. What do you suppose Mordecai meant in Esther 4:14, when he talked about "enlargement and deliverance" coming to the Jews from some other place, in the event that Esther chose not to become involved?

3. What is the difference between a "professing faith" and a "productive faith"?

4. What kinds of challenges to a "productive faith" have you been faced with in your own community? How have you responded?

For Further Reading

Schaeffer, Francis A. *A Christian Manifesto.* Westchester, Ill.: Crossway Books, 1981.

Whitehead, John W. *The Second American Revolution.* Elgin, Ill.: David C. Cook Publishing Co., 1982.

2

A Place to Stand

A Foundation for Our World

You may remember, as a very young child, being fascinated by a picture of Atlas holding the world on his shoulders. Perhaps you found it remarkable that the ancient Greeks, at least for a time, found this image an altogether satisfactory representation of how the world was sustained. Here was this ideally formed man, the strongest of the strong, shouldering the earth and holding it in place for the men, women, and other creatures making their homes there. It must have given great comfort to generations of true believers at that time to know that so reliable a foundation had been set beneath them.

But did you ever stop to consider this one puzzling thing: What was Atlas standing on? What was supporting him as he faithfully performed his duties? And why did it not occur to those ancient Greeks that their hero's great strength would avail them not a whit unless a solid foundation was under Atlas?

Apparently, however, someone must have had similar thoughts at some time or another, for the image of Atlas holding the world on his shoulders was ultimately abandoned by thinking people of the day. Evidently, someone among them dared to ask the logical question that the popular image of Atlas certainly must have evoked: Can we be certain that there is an absolutely reliable place for the sustainer of our world to stand? In other words, how can we know that this foundational belief, this world view we have chosen, is true? The inability to give a satisfactory answer to this question soon spelled the downfall of the Atlas myth.

In many ways our age is faced with the same sort of situation. All around us are prophets of change, oracles of hope, purveyors of prosperity, each with a different program or scheme for making the world a better place to live. Each has his or her own vision of the shoulders that must hold our world in place. All are prepared to argue and work for their own particular understanding to bring it to fruition in our day. For some, that vision is of a world sustained by the strength of increasing material prosperity for all. The shoulders holding the world in place for such people are those of the free market and illimitable natural and human resources. For others, the Atlas needed today is that of the all-powerful central government, upon whose shoulders the men and women of our land will be guaranteed work, prosperity, and happiness. For others still, the ancient image finds expression in a feverish laboring for the classless society, the confiscation of the means of production, distribution, and exchange in the name of the proletariat. Indeed, there is seemingly no end to the wide variety of interpretations as to how best to hold the world and its people in a stable and trustworthy place.

Yet, to each of these views of our world we must ask the question raised by that anonymous Greek so many years ago: How can we be certain that there is an absolutely reliable foundation upon which to base this understanding? And, if there is none, how can thinking people be expected to commit themselves to something so tenuous and uncertain?

The Foundation of Scripture

In our day the world needs a place on which to stand, a perspective on the universe and life itself that is altogether reliable and sure. We need a vantage point from which to look out on the problems and challenges of the day and begin to initiate changes with the certainty that they will eventuate in positive and lasting results. The true world changers of our day will be those who have an absolute ground on which to stand, and such a ground is available only to those who look for it within the pages of the Word of God. Since it is the Bible and the Bible alone that provides an absolute starting point for changing the world, it must be upon the great pages of the Book that the world changers of our day take their stand.

Students of the Scriptures find therein a description of the world and life that is breathtaking in its scope, wonderful in its complexity, and yet profound in its simplicity. Here is described an awesome view of the universe, which the sovereign God, out of the infinitude of His grace, brings into being for the glory of His own name and the well-being and prosperity of the creatures He has made. We understand from the Scriptures that the universe is orderly, beautiful, marvelous, infinitely complex, diverse on a grand scale, and filled with wonder at every turn. Yet, it is dependent upon and harmonizes together for the majestic glory of the God who brought it into being. In this place of unspeakable beauty and wonder, God has introduced rational creatures who are able to know Him and to enter into fellowship with Him. For them He has organized the world, and subjected it to their governance. For their well-being He has ordained it. And, in obedience to Him, they find their greatest happiness and their only lasting joy and peace.

Humans, however, being weak and finite, cannot avoid the temptation to be as God, and thus they have fallen from their sinless state into a condition of rebellion and wretchedness. They become enemies of the God who has made them and given them life. They come to despise His ways and to ignore His Word—and they reject His free offer of restoration and wholeness through the provision He has made in Jesus Christ.

Some, by the free grace of God, come to find the redemption that He has for them. Through faith they understand the significance of the cross and receive the living Lord Jesus Christ into their hearts and lives. They are born again into the family of God. They become such as long for His fellowship and dwell in His Spirit. They revel in the joys of prayer and worship, seeking wholeheartedly to serve Him with their lives. And they understand the truth of our assertion that only the Word of God can provide the certainty and the place to stand, which our generation so desperately needs. These are the true world changers, and they are even now being raised up in our midst by the scores of thousands, in order to bring the life-changing message of the grace of God to the men and women of this age.

But some may reply, and, indeed, we should expect it to be so, by demanding of us what certainty we can have of these assertions. How can *we* know that the Bible is the reliable place to stand that we claim it to be? What absolute assurances do we possess?

This is the critical question before us. We who would change the world and have the Bible as the starting point for our efforts must be able to answer this challenge. For, unless we have absolute confidence in the reliability of the Bible, we shall never be able either to convince a skeptical generation of its trustworthiness or to make significant progress in changing the world according to biblical guidelines.

Where, then, does our certainty come from? How can we know that the Bible can be trusted as a dependable basis for changing the world in our day?

The Reliability of Scripture

In response to this challenge we make four important observations. These provide the foundation for our confidence in the trustworthiness of the Scriptures.

1. *The Bible claims for itself a place of absolute reliability.* It makes bold assertions about its trustworthiness, inviting men to depend on its sayings and to dwell within its parameters.

For example, the Bible claims that it is "a lamp unto my feet, and a light unto my path" (Ps. 119:105). It claims to be the beacon by which we find our way in this world. Moreover, the Scriptures claim to be the light in which we see all other light (Ps. 36:9), that is, the means whereby all true understanding is revealed. It is the Word of God, which is not to be added to or detracted from but kept in sincerity and truth by the generations of those who would know God (Deut. 4:2). It is the Bible in which we are to meditate and abide in order to find our prosperity and our peace (Josh. 1:8). Moreover, Scripture claims that "the law of the LORD is perfect, converting the soul: the testimony of the LORD is sure, making wise the simple" (Ps. 19:7). We are told that "every word of God is pure . . ." (Prov. 30:5). It is the words of God and of His Son Jesus Christ that give life (John 6:63). These are the words breathed of God Himself, given by His Holy Spirit, and useful for every good work (2 Tim.

3:15, 17; 2 Pet. 1:21). Indeed, the Word of God itself is to be our very life, so certain are its truths, so reliable its teachings (Matt. 4:4).

No contemporary philosophy, no school of political thought, and no movement for reform of any kind dares to make such sweeping and bold assertions. Not even modern evolutionary science will claim for itself any more abiding validity than a relativity of truth, bound to a particular time, a particular place, and a particular combination of events. Only the Word of God dares to make such claims for itself of certainty and truth, for only that Word has come from the very heart and mind of God Himself. Thus it cannot *but* be the altogether true and reliable expression of His will for our lives in the world. Our confidence in the reliability of the Bible derives in the first place from its own bold claims for certainty and absolute truth.

2. *We have confidence in the Word of God because of its prophetic reliability.* We can see this especially with respect to the prophecies concerning the Lord Jesus Christ.

Throughout the Old Testament there are clear indications that God planned to send a Savior for His people, in order to bring them back into a proper relationship with Himself. In many prophetic passages the Word of God speaks about the Christ who is to come. These prophecies, given hundreds of years before the events of the life of Jesus, were meant to enable God's people to identify the Messiah when He finally came. However, they have another benefit for us who stand beyond the cross in the flow of history. These prophecies not only confirm for us the ministry of our Lord Jesus Christ; they also convince us of the reliability of the Scriptures. If the Bible shows itself trustworthy in the area of prophecy, we feel we can trust it in all other areas of life as well.

There are, for example, prophecies concerning the birth of Jesus Christ. Isaiah 7:14 tells us that He would be born of a virgin and that He would be called Immanuel (cf. Luke 1:26-33; Matt. 1:23). Micah tells us (5:2) that He would be born in Bethlehem (cf. Luke 2:1-7). And we know that He was to have been born before the destruction of the second temple in Jerusalem, according to Malachi 3:1. Since the second temple was destroyed by the legions of Titus in A.D. 70, the Messiah had to have come before then.

There are, further, prophecies concerning the peculiar ministry of the Messiah. We are told that it would involve preaching good news from God (Isa. 61:1), healing the sick (Isa. 42:7), and taking away the sins of God's people (Isa. 53:5-6). We are told that He would initiate a kingdom and a reign that would know no end (Isa. 9:6-7).

And we know certain things from prophecy concerning His death. We know that it was to have been accomplished on a cross (Ps. 22) and that it was as an offering for sin (Isa. 53:5-6). And we know that Christ's death was to be followed by His burial in the grave of a rich man and then a powerful resurrection from the dead (Isa. 53:9-10).

All these things and many, many more were fulfilled in the life of Jesus Christ, precisely as the Scriptures foretold. And we have confidence that if the Scriptures could be so reliable and trustworthy in this most difficult and challenging area of truth, we can trust them for all they teach us concerning our lives in this world. The prophetic reliability of the Word of God serves to convince us that it offers a certain place for us to stand in these days.

3. *We are convinced of the absolute reliability of the Scriptures when we compare their teaching with any other world and life view that exists today or ever has come before.* The superiority of the biblical view of life over any other view can be seen in the glaring inconsistencies of nonbiblical world views and their inevitable tendency to deny the basic truths of their own positions and ultimately depend upon the truth as the Bible presents it.

This can be seen, for instance, by a brief examination of the general evolutionary view of human life in the cosmos. The evolutionist insists that we live in a totally material universe, one without any metaphysical realities, that is, one where there is no God. Everything we see today, we are told, derives from the chance explosion of cosmic matter aeons ago and the ultimate gradual development of the universe and the life within it. Everything that exists, including human life, is the ultimate product of time plus matter plus chance. There is no meaning, no purpose, no reason for life, since life is simply the chance product of atomic collisions and the random combination of chemicals, minerals, and protein.

Yet, in the midst of this cosmic confusion, the evolutionist is involved in a feverish search for meaning and order. And it is in this search that the internal inconsistencies of his world view begin to become obvious.

In the first place, the evolutionist wants to insist the universe is governed by something called chance, an unpredictable, unknowable, uncertain something or other that intervenes in the affairs of the cosmos to bring about changes both subtle and profound. At the same time, however, the evolutionist wants to believe there is order in the universe and there are laws to be discovered and used in order to make the world a better place in which to live. Thus, evolutionists undertake frenzied scientific research aimed at discovering the inner workings of the cosmos, so as to be better able to master its elements for their own purposes.

Now where did this lust for order and control come from? Certainly not from the evolutionist's own cosmology, for he has already told us in no uncertain terms that the chance-governed universe is unknowable, uncertain, and unpredictable. Yet, in his labors as a scientist, he first denies those assumptions, then works upon the basis of some organizing principles that sound as though they might have come from the Christian world and life view. In fact, the evolutionist, having been made in the image of God, cannot deny his need of truth as God has defined it. In his most fundamental labors, the evolutionist is forced to deny his own faulty premises and to operate on the basis of biblical truths, although he will never admit that this is, in fact, what he is about.

Again, when it comes to his view of man, the evolutionist is not consistent with his own basic organizing principles. He insists that there is no meaning or purpose to the elements of the cosmos. Even man is not truly significant, being nothing more than the chance product of a random combining of a few primary substances millions of years ago. On that basis it is absurd to speak of there being meaning of any absolute kind in the universe.

Yet, in the day-to-day practical affairs of his life and work, the evolutionist appears totally convinced that there is something meaningful about mankind. He loves and wants to be loved. He enjoys his work and thinks about himself and his world and longs for a better life. The evolutionist, too, suffers with the suffering and despises tyrants of the earth. He has an inborn sense of the dignity and importance of man, a sense not to be found within the parameters of his evolutionary world view. Rather, those sentiments concerning the human condition well up from within his innermost being, where the image of God keeps reminding him of who and what he really is.

In a hundred other ways the evolutionary scientist shows the instability of his own basic view of the world and life and the contrasting reliability of those truths deriving from a biblical world view. For this reason, we can have confidence that the understanding of man's place in the world presented within the pages of the Word of God is a reliable place for us to take our stand.

4. *We would observe that all those who have come to trust in the Lord Jesus Christ and to accept the view of truth that He sets forth in the Word of God have received the gift of the Holy Spirit.* He has given us newness of life in Christ. He is developing within us the gifts and virtues that mark us off as peculiar people unto the Lord. And He convinces us in our hearts that the Word of God is altogether true and reliable. In the end it is only the convincing power of the Holy Spirit that provides us with the certainty we need in order to be able to put down our full weight on the Bible. Jesus said of Him, "Howbeit when he, the Spirit of truth, is come, he will guide you into all truth: for he shall not speak of himself; but whatsoever he shall hear, that shall he speak . . ." (John 16:13).

Because we have the Spirit of God living in us, testifying to our hearts of the trustworthiness of the Scriptures, we can be certain *by faith* that the Bible is a reliable place for us to stand. Let us stand, therefore, as those who are fully confident that we have within our grasp the understandings necessary to begin changing our world according to the will and pleasure of God.

The Implications of Our Biblical Foundation

But what does this mean for us as individuals? What is the personal significance to each one of us when the Bible is found as a trustworthy guide and starting place?

Several things need to be said here. In the first place, each one of us must recognize and accept our individual responsibility to start becoming more familiar with the teachings of the Word of God. Biblical ignorance is one of the greatest sins that a Christian world changer can commit. We must determine that we are going to spend time, a great deal of time, getting to know the contents and teachings of the Word of God. Only when the Scriptures have begun to saturate our minds will they begin to have their molding effect upon our lives. We must resolve to read, study, and begin memorizing more of the Bible than ever before. It must become our daily discipline. As Job of old, we must come to the place where we are able to say, ". . . I have esteemed the words of his mouth more than my necessary food" (Job 23:12).

How is it with you, friend? Have you availed yourself of the Word of God as often and as thoroughly as you ought? We cannot expect to play an active and effective part in changing our world unless we have first determined to master the manual that God has given to guide our efforts. Today is the day to renew our commitment to the Word of God as the only trustworthy place on which to take our stand.

Second, once we have begun to master the Word of God, we must make certain that it, in turn, is beginning to master us. Study and memorizing of the Bible will do us no good if we do not allow the Bible to exert an actual formative influence on our lives. We must determine to let the Bible be our guide, its Author our Lord indeed.

This involves critically examining our lives day in and day out to see if there are any things therein that are displeasing to the Lord and contrary to what we are discovering in His truth. As we are enabled by the Holy Spirit to identify these tendencies, we must repent of them and beseech God for the power to have His will work itself out in our lives. We must labor after obedience in the whole of existence, in our attitudes, our work, our relationships, and every other facet of our being in the world. Only then will the power of the Word of God, the power to be that blessed place to stand, begin to be felt in our lives. And only then will we be truly effective as world changers for our Lord.

Next, we must develop the ability to cast a scriptural eye on the world around us. We must learn, as John Calvin suggested, to let the Bible be the spectacles through which we look out on the whole of human life. We must cultivate the ability to ask serious questions, which our generation needs to ask if we are to find our way out of the morass of sin and relativism into which the secular world leadership has plunged us. As we truly know what the Bible has to say about the whole of human life, we must concern ourselves with the scriptural teachings on such matters as government, education, economics, the family, and interpersonal relationships. Only when we have begun to understand that the Word of God is relevant to all these areas and more, and only when we have started to develop the critical capacity for seeing our world through the eyes, as it were, of God Himself, will we be able to describe solutions to the world's ills—solutions consistent with the mind of God as it is revealed in the pages of Holy Writ. The challenge is awesome, and the responsibility is staggering. But if our world is ever to experience the blessedness of God's truth over its every dimension of life, it will only be as you and I commit ourselves to the necessary praying, studying, thinking, and acting that will lay a biblical foundation for building a better world.

Finally, we must determine to begin taking specific steps to declare and show how the biblical world and life view stands in stark contrast to the prevailing systems. As we become more informed about the teachings of Scripture, more obedient in the whole of our lives, and more aware of its potential to mold the whole of life around us, we must begin to assert for others to see and hear what the specific requirements of God's Holy Word are for our generation. In doing this we become like the prophets of old, who stood boldly before the people of their day and declared, "Thus saith the Lord."

We must commit ourselves to specific actions for setting forth the truth of God's Word for this generation to see, and we must begin at once! We must share the teachings of God's Word in our conversations with family, neighbors, and friends. We must become active participants in classes where the Scriptures are studied seriously and where the learners look to one another for additional insights and understanding. We must protest ungodliness and untruth on the solid basis of biblical teachings. This we can do, for example, through letters to editors of magazines and newspapers and to television networks regarding programming, petitions to our lawmakers, public rallies, editorial replies, picketing, and a host of other specific ways.

We must untiringly determine to force the issue of biblical

truth upon a generation that has no firm base on which to stand. Only thus will we be able to convince some of them of the trustworthiness of the scriptural world and life view.

There is a world to be changed, and the responsibility for beginning to change it rests squarely upon the shoulders of those who name the name of Jesus Christ upon themselves. *We can change the world to show forth the beauty and holiness of God once again!* But we must come to see that this Atlasian task can only be accomplished upon the starting place of a biblical world and life view. The Scriptures are our place to stand. Let us stand, therefore, and begin together to labor for the changes that alone can bring the blessings of God and His truth to ourselves and our fellowmen.

Questions for Study or Discussion

1. Take a few moments just now to describe in writing or discuss with a friend what your personal Bible reading and study habits are. Are these adequate for you to take your place as a world changer?

2. How would you define the importance of each of the following passages for the role of Scripture in our everyday lives?

Matthew 22:29—

John 6:63—

Ephesians 2:19–20—

2 Peter 1:19–21—

3. What would you like to see as the ideal pattern of Bible reading and study for your own life?

For Further Reading

Lindsell, Harold. *The Battle for the Bible.* Grand Rapids, Mich.: Zondervan, 1976.

Moore, T. M. *Plant a Seed . . . and Watch It Grow!* Evangelism Explosion, P.O. Box 23820, Fort Lauderdale, FL 33307.

Sproul, R. C. *Knowing Scripture.* Downers Grove, Ill.: IVP, 1977.

3

A Changed Heart for a Changed Nation

The Place to Begin

The first disciples were described by their contemporaries as those who had "turned the world upside down" (Acts 17:6). They were the kind of people who made things happen. They realized that the truth, as they had come to understand and embrace it, demanded allegiance in the whole of their lives. Having come to know Jesus Christ in the newness of life, they could not simply sit around doing nothing. The Spirit within them compelled them to change their world. So profound was the impact they were able to make in communities all across the Roman Empire that those who observed their world-changing efforts could think of no better way to describe what they saw. The early Christians literally stood the world on its ear!

We need a similar effort today. If ever there was an age in which the world and the people in it needed a new beginning, surely it is ours. And the indications are that the conditions are right for today's believers to succeed in a manner more dramatic and far-reaching than has been seen in history since those earliest days of the Christian church. We can change the world, and we must begin to take the necessary steps at once.

But where do we begin? How do we determine the priorities for meeting the needs and overcoming the tremendous problems before us in our time? How do we get started in the awesome

41

task of bringing the saving and renewing truth of God's love in Jesus Christ into the totality of human experience? How do we begin to get a handle on such a monumental undertaking?

The place to begin to change the world is both the easiest and the hardest task before us. It is easy, because it requires only that we be willing to share a simple but profound message with the men and women of our generation. Yet, it is difficult, because the response it requires is so all-encompassing that nothing short of a miracle of God can bring it about.

Furthermore, the base from which we begin to change the world is also the place to which we must continually return if our total effort is to succeed. Without a mighty initiative and an ongoing commitment, we shall never succeed in the critical assignment of bringing lasting change into our world.

Most importantly, however, we must understand from the beginning that in our world-changing undertaking we are guaranteed success. We can be absolutely certain that positive and lasting results will come from our efforts in this most important area.

The place to begin changing the world is on the inside, within the hearts and minds of men and women. For unless we are able to do something about the motivations, desires, perspectives, and goals of the people who make up the communities of our world, any other changes we might be able to introduce will be merely cosmetic and temporary at best. Permanent change begins on the inside. Unless we are first of all and continuously concentrating our efforts on changing men and women from the inside out, we will be certain to fail in our long-range desires of changing the world. No amount of political activism or educational reform and no legislative or judicial enactment will yield any abiding fruit without this first most important matter being addressed by all concerned.

How do we propose to accomplish such change?

Nearly two thousand years ago, Jesus Christ stood on a hill in Galilee and presented His disciples with His plan for bringing permanent, positive change into the world. As He surveyed the ages and considered the problems and needs of men and women from all nations, tribes, and generations, He concluded that there was one primary solution, which all would require: "Go ye therefore, and teach all nations, baptizing them in the name of the Father, and of the Son, and of the Holy Ghost: Teaching them to observe all things whatsoever I have commanded you: and, lo, I am with you alway, even unto the end of the world" (Matt. 28:19–20).

This first and continuous step, this easiest and hardest task, this undertaking guaranteed to begin the process of changing our world from the inside out, is the sharing with our neighbors and friends of the wonderful story of the gospel of Jesus Christ. Without this most important effort on the part of each and every one of us, we will most certainly *not* be able to change the world in our time.

A Challenge for All of Us

Each of us must become committed to the task of telling the story of God's saving love in Jesus Christ to the people we meet each day. We must pledge our support for efforts to publish God's Good News among all men and nations. Jesus Christ has given us newness of life through His saving life, death, and resurrection. And we are the only people alive today who understand the tremendous significance of what He has done. If we fail to share the love of Jesus Christ with our neighbors, how shall they ever learn of it? How shall they ever find the peace that passes understanding, the joy unutterable, the purpose that impels us into concerted effort to change the world, unless they first hear from us the Good News of God's love in Jesus Christ?

There are not enough preachers to tell the whole world, and the largest percentage of the world's population never places itself in a location where it might hear one of those preachers anyway. Someone must go to these lost friends. Someone must tell them of Jesus' love. Someone must help them find the life-changing power that can make all things new, that can deliver them into a quality of living that is beyond comparison, and that can fill their daily lives with new meaning and joy.

Shortly after his inauguration, President Reagan is reported to have met with his cabinet and staff to discuss the utter importance of their committing themselves to a course of action designed to rescue America from the doldrums of moral and economic stagnation into which she had drifted. As the discussion progressed and the questions and doubts began to be voiced, the president looked at his colleagues and said simply, "If not us, who? If not now, when?"

Christian friend, the same questions can be put to you and me. When it comes to sharing with our lost friends and neighbors the only truth that can rescue them from misery, despair, and meaninglessness, "If not us, who? If not now, when?"

We must commit ourselves to the task of changing our world from the inside out.

It will help us in this effort if we make certain first of all that we fully understand the gospel of Jesus Christ. We need to be sure that we grasp it in all its comprehensiveness and uniqueness. We need to see it as the God-given gift that it is before we can share it with others.

Further, we need to know something about the people around us. We need to understand their problems and to sympathize with their hurts. We need to be able to communicate God's Good News to them in a manner that is easy for them to understand.

Finally, we need to be able to share forthrightly and clearly the story of Jesus' love in an effective presentation of the gospel. Although we may know full well what God has done for lost sinners and may have the clearest of understandings about the people around us, unless we can take that message to them in an effective and concise manner, we shall be unable to succeed at this most important point.

Understanding the Gospel

The gospel of Jesus Christ is not a fairy tale, nor philosophy, nor merely another of the world's great religions. It is, in fact, the best-attested historical fact of all time. This is the crucial point to keep clear: *The gospel of Jesus Christ is a fact of human history.* Witnessed by hundreds of people, it was irrefutable in its day by even its most ardent foes. And it was recorded by contemporaries in written documents, hundreds of which exist to this day. The fact that secular historians have chosen to neglect or denigrate this incredible series of events does not render the happenings themselves any less historical in nature. The people, places, circumstances, and consequences of the story of the life, death, and resurrection of Jesus Christ are events of human history. And, as such, they constitute the most remarkable truth that can ever be told—the only truth that can change the world.

The gospel is the story of the unfathomable love of God, who, in the person of His Son Jesus Christ, has opened a road to salvation, a way of hope, peace, joy, purpose, forgiveness, and victory over sin for all those who will put their trust in what He did on the cross and in His resurrection from the dead.

The gospel offers a way of life so powerful and so comprehensive that those who are its possessors can accurately be described as having been "born again," and those who do not have it can effectively be characterized as "lost."

It is a story that has become so important to each of us who knows Jesus Christ in a personal way. We know that He has forgiven our sins because we believe that His death on the cross was for us. We know that He has purchased a place for us in heaven because we believe that He rose from the dead and gained the victory over death and Satan. And we know that He has given us a new life of purpose and hope because we know that His Spirit has come to live in us by faith.

Since we know that this gospel has the power to change our world from the inside out, we also understand the importance of sharing this wonderful story with the people around us. As surely as the gospel has changed our lives, it can change theirs as well. As surely as the love of Jesus Christ has quickened in us the desire to be world changers in our generation, it can do it for our neighbors as well.

The gospel can "turn the world upside down," change it from inside out.

Understanding Our Neighbors

It will help us in our sharing the gospel with our neighbors if we know some things about them. What is on their minds as they think about the really important matters in their lives? What kinds of information do they seek in the normal course of a day? What appeals to them, what are their needs, how do they perceive the problems of our world?

Only in some ways is ours a unique generation. For the most part, we are like all the ages that have come and gone before. As the writer of Ecclesiastes noted, "There is nothing new under the sun." The same problems, fears, desires, distractions, and amusements that have occupied men and women throughout history are of concern to the people in our generation. They are interested in earning a living, getting ahead, raising a family, gaining esteem, enjoying the fruits of their labors, finding meaning and purpose for their lives. These concerns will be present in a unique combination of priorities with each person we meet. It is our responsibility to take the time to get to know our neighbors well enough to begin to understand their concerns and to show how God's Good News can bring richness and purpose to their lives.

Thus, the burden is on us as Good News bearers to become informed about the critical issues of our day and how these issues impact upon our neighbors. Our challenge is to reach out in love, to make friends, and to care. It is our responsibility to initiate and sustain new relationships, new conversations, and new involvements that are going to enable us to get to know the people of our age so that we can tell them of Jesus' love.

Jesus said that He had come to *seek* and to save the lost. He did not simply wait around for people to come to Him. See Him talking to the woman at the well in Sychar, how He understands her need, and how gently He leads her to consider His claims. See Him comforting the parents of the child who had died, as His heart aches with their pain. How tenderly He must have touched both parents and child as He brought her back to life. See Him walking the width and breadth of the land—healing, teaching, helping, and loving with a love that could have come only from God. And, in the midst of it all, hear Him talking of the kingdom that was at hand. Hear Him calling His generation to repentance and faith. Surely here was the One who understood the age-old problems of the people of His day and who reached out to one and all with the Good News of God's forgiveness and love. As the Father sent Jesus into the world, so He has sent us. We are the ones who must reach out in our day to make the gospel relevant to the needs of people around us.

But how shall we share it? How can we make this Good News known?

Sharing God's Good News

This is a question that in the early days of my ministry haunted me as few things I had ever known. I realized that God had called me into the ministry to bring His Good News to the lost. Yet, I was just one person and scarcely knew where to begin to tell others about Jesus Christ. How could I possibly hope to fulfill my calling in life? But God is faithful, and He will not give us a task which He does not intend to enable us to perform. In my case, it was through the patience and wisdom of a minister friend that I came to learn how to share my faith with others. He showed me a simple but effective way of telling others about Jesus Christ and of teaching that skill to others. I began to teach that skill to others. As I began to teach that skill to members of our church, other congregations saw the number of people who were being won to Christ here and asked if we could share with them our evangelism methods. Year after year more people were trained through this program, until today it has grown into the ministry of Evangelism Explosion III International. From one pastor's evangelizing and teaching his congregation, this exciting work has developed into an international, interdenominational ministry spanning 50 nations, and over 6,000 churches. Scores of thousands of lay men and women are sharing their faith, leading others to the change from the inside out that makes all the difference in people's lives.

In the ministry of Evangelism Explosion we have developed a very simple and effective way of sharing the message of God's love. It consists of an outline comprising five major points, each of which flows logically from the first. Those five points are as follows:

1. Grace
2. Man
3. God
4. Christ
5. Faith

These five words represent the main ideas to be shared with anyone who needs to know the love of God. Take a moment and say them out loud: GRACE, MAN, GOD, CHRIST, FAITH. Say them again: GRACE, MAN, GOD, CHRIST, FAITH. Now close your eyes and say them again.

Once you have mastered the order of these five basic points, you can begin to add under each one of them the qualifying statements that will begin to bring real meaning into your presentation of the gospel.

Let's start with GRACE:

1. **Grace**
    a) *Heaven is a free gift.*
    b) *It is not earned or deserved.*

This is the starting point for sharing the gospel. Note that it is a positive concept. We start the message of God's love from the end result, heaven. We direct our friends' focus toward what God wants to give them right away.

Notice also that this is a fairly startling idea, at least it will be for many of the people with whom you will be sharing it. Most people think heaven is something you earn by being "good"—going to church, singing in the choir, teaching Sunday school, and so on. But the fact of the matter is that heaven is a free gift; it is not earned or deserved. "For by grace are ye saved; through faith; it is the gift of God: Not of works, lest any man should boast" (Eph. 2:8–9).

Now let's look at what the gospel says about MAN:

2. **Man**
    a) *Is a sinner.*
    b) *Cannot save himself.*

That seems pretty clear. Man has broken God's law. He is a sinner, and so nothing he might try to do could ever make him good enough to *earn* a place in heaven. "For all have sinned, and fallen short of the glory of God" (Rom. 3:23).

The importance of this comes through when you share what the gospel says about GOD:

3. **God**
    a) *God is merciful.*
    b) *God is just.*

God is merciful. He wants us to be with Him in heaven. He wants His creatures to have eternal life. But He is also just. This means that He has to judge our sins. They have to be paid for if His justice is to be satisfied. Although God has loved us "with an everlasting love" (Jer. 31:3), He is "of purer eyes than to behold evil" (Hab. 1:13) and "will by no means clear the guilty" (Exod. 34:7).

This is where CHRIST comes in:

4. Christ
a) *Who He is: The infinite-eternal God-man.*
b) *What He did: Died on a cross to purchase a place for us in heaven.*

God's love is clearly seen in Jesus, who became a man though He is the eternal God. And He died on a cross though He was sinless. He died to pay for sins, *our* sins. In this He shows God's love and fulfills God's justice. He died so that we do not have to. "And the Word was made flesh, and dwelt among us" (John 1:14). God "hath made him to be sin for us" (2 Cor. 5:21) so that we might be forgiven.

Now that Christ has risen from the dead, He offers eternal life to anyone who will receive it by FAITH:

5. Faith
a) *What it is not: Intellectual assent or temporal belief.*
b) *What it is: Trusting in Jesus Christ alone.*

Faith is the key to heaven. But faith is not mere intellectual assent, mere knowledge about Jesus Christ. Nor is it simply trusting God for things such as safety, health, wealth, and so on, all of which are temporal and will one day pass away.

Saving faith is *trusting*—trusting in Jesus Christ alone for our salvation. Only as we depend totally on Him can we know that God has forgiven us and made us new. "Believe on the Lord Jesus Christ, and thou shalt be saved" (Acts 16:31).

This, then, is the gospel message:

1. Grace
a) *Heaven is a free gift.*
b) *It is not earned or deserved* (Eph. 2:8–9).

2. Man
a) *Is a sinner.*
b) *Cannot save himself* (Rom. 3:23).

3. God
a) *Is merciful.*
b) *Is just* (Jer. 31:3; Hab. 1:13; Exod. 34:7).

4. Christ
a) *Who He is: The infinite-eternal God-man.*
b) *What He did: Died on a cross to purchase a place for us in heaven* (John 1:14; 2 Cor. 5:21).

5. **Faith**
a) *What it is not: Intellectual assent or temporal belief.*
b) *What it is: Trusting in Jesus Christ alone* (Acts 16:31).

Go back and read that brief outline out loud two or three times. See how logically it flows? It makes sense because you and I have come to embrace the truth it contains. And you can become an effective communicator of the gospel by using just such a brief outline as this. As you work at memorizing it, you will come to see more clearly how each part of the gospel is a truth you hold dear. It is a part of your very life. Practice it often. You will soon be able to say this outline in your own words.

Practice saying it out loud as often as you think of it. Meditate daily on the great truths of each point. Ask some Christian friend to listen to you say it. Then, talk it through with your Christian friends and family members, embellishing the outline in your own words until you become comfortable with each part.

Next, begin asking God to lead you to people who need to hear this great truth. Because you know that God has promised to bring people to Himself when we share the gospel, you can go with confidence. He has promised that His Word would not return to Him void (Isa. 55:11). Moses was a stutterer, but God used him in a mighty way to proclaim His truth. Paul did not consider himself eloquent of speech, but God blessed his faithfulness. We may perceive ourselves to be the feeblest of communicators, but because the truth we have to share is so powerful, God will often honor our faithfulness in leading others to Christ as we tell them of His Good News.

But we must tell them. We must reach out in the love of God to share this life-changing message with everyone around us. Only then will we be able to change the world from the inside out.

Many of those whom we tell of the gospel will want to accept Jesus Christ as their Lord and Savior. We can help them to do that by leading them, phrase by phrase, in a simple prayer such as this:

Lord Jesus, I need You. Thank You for dying for my sins. I repent of them now and want my life to count for You. Come into my heart and make me new. Amen.

This simple prayer can be the entry way to an entirely new life.

And only we—you and I and everyone else who loves Jesus Christ supremely—have the ability to tell others about Him. For we are the only ones who have been entrusted with this great story. *We must not fail.*

Guidelines for Witnessing

Shortly after the apostle Paul came away from the city which had remarked that the disciples were turning the world upside down, he arrived in Athens. His behavior there presents a pattern which is instructive for each one of us who is determined to be a bearer of God's Good News to the men and women of our generation. As we look at Paul's moving and sharing among the citizens of Athens, five principles for developing an evangelistic way of life present themselves for our consideration.

First, notice that Paul did not wait for the Athenians to come to him. He had learned well the lesson of the Lord Jesus about seeking out those who needed to hear the gospel. We are told that he went to the synagogue and the marketplace, key centers where the people were (Acts 17:17). Paul knew that he would never change his world if he waited for the world to come to him. So he went where the people were and took the initiative to tell them about Jesus.

We know where the people are—in our neighborhoods, in the stores and shops of our cities, in offices, laundromats, schools, social clubs, and a thousand other places. Since these people are not going to come to us to ask if we have heard any good news lately, we must commit ourselves to going to them. Each day we must ask God to bring to mind the places we will be going and the people we are likely to see. We must pray that He will give us boldness and clarity of speech to tell them the Good News of His love. Then we must share with our friends, neighbors, and associates in the course of our conversation and our lives the wonderful story of what God has accomplished in Jesus Christ.

Second, see how Paul started on a positive note when he wanted to talk about Jesus. He did not chide the Athenians for their foolishness and sin. He actually complimented them for being so intensely religious (Acts 17:22). Since Paul wanted

them to know that it was good for them to want to know about
God, he commended them for their zeal in religious matters.

You and I can also begin on a positive note to help others find
the truth about Jesus. We can always find something genuinely
complimentary to say about the people we meet. Because our
message begins on a positive note, we will want to start by having established a positive atmosphere in our conversation. We
do not need to judge or criticize. We need to look for something
that is genuinely praiseworthy and commendable, which will
enable us to begin our conversation on a positive note. Only
thus will we be able to demonstrate the love of God that we
want so badly for them to understand in what we are about to
share.

Third, it is interesting that Paul was careful to share the Good
News of Jesus Christ in language with which his audience could
identify. In this case, Paul spoke to them in the language of
philosophy. He was addressing an audience of philosophers,
people who liked to spend their time thinking about the ultimate
composition and purpose of things. They took this very seriously. It was on their minds constantly.

Thus, when Paul was looking for some common point of contact, some identifying concepts that might link what he had to
say with what these people had on their minds, he turned to
Greek philosophy. The two quotes in verse 28 of this passage are
from Greek philosophers of the pre-Christian era. Paul was inti-
mating that the great questions that have occupied the minds of
thinkers down through the ages find their resolution in Jesus
Christ. It was a way of communicating the gospel with which his
audience could clearly identify.

The same burden of responsibility is upon us today. Although
we may not need to understand a great deal of Greek philosophy, we do want to be able to talk about the meaning of the
gospel for the people of our generation. What does the gospel
mean for one who is fearful? What can it do in the life of one
who is filled with hate? Has the gospel any power to deliver from
alcohol? Drugs? Lust? Materialism? How does the gospel bring
new meaning and love to human relationships?

Only as we study to understand the great concerns of our
generation and what the gospel can accomplish in meeting the
needs of our day will we be able to couch our communications

of God's Good News in terms that will be truly meaningful for the people around us. We must resolve to share the gospel with them at their level and according to their needs, so that they will be able to accept its truths more readily.

Fourth, we must be careful that we mince no words when it comes to the truths of the Bible. Although Paul was talking to his audience in the language of Greek philosophy, when it came to what the Word of God requires of all men, Paul "told it like it is." In verses 30 and 31 Paul is very clear about what the gospel requires in terms of repentance and the Lordship of Jesus Christ. He did not merely tell his audience that they ought to start going to church, or even that they should simply follow the example of Jesus. He told them to acknowledge Him as Judge and Lord. He was perfectly clear on what God requires, and so must you and I be.

In our sharing of the gospel there will be a temptation to try to make it palatable to our listeners. We will be tempted to tone it down, to talk about "good Christian living," and to leave off the need for repentance and a genuine saving faith in the Lord Jesus Christ. *We must fight this temptation, for it arises from fear and doubt.* We must clearly state the eternal truths of the gospel without compromise or confusion. Only thus will we be able to make God's love perfectly known among the men and women of our world.

Finally, we must see that such aggressive, sensitive, and clear communicating of the gospel produces mixed results. Paul had some who mocked him (v. 32). They considered what he had to say as totally ridiculous and wanted nothing to do with him. *But at least they had heard what God wanted them to know.* At least the substance of the gospel had fallen upon their ears.

But there were also many who followed Paul, accepting what he had to say (v. 34). They believed him and acknowledged Jesus Christ as their Savior and Lord. They entered into the life-changing, world-changing sphere of those who had come to know Jesus in a personal way.

And we must expect similar results as well. We must go forth to share our faith, expecting that on the one hand there will be those who reject our message. We might be laughed at or avoided, but it will be because of the gospel we bring and not because of us personally.

But on the other hand there will be those who will literally be eternally grateful that we took the time to tell them about the Lord Jesus. For, through our sharing the gospel with them, they will come to understand the love of God for the first time. They will experience His cleansing and forgiveness from within. They will pass from mere mortal existence into everlasting life. And this will happen because you and I took the time to reach out to them with the love of God and His Good News.

You can be used of God to lead many, many people into a saving relationship with Jesus Christ. All over the world today literally hundreds of thousands of people just like you and I are sharing their faith in Jesus Christ with the men and women of their communities. But we need hundreds and thousands and millions more just like them. We need you to determine that you will be among those world changers who have committed themselves to bringing lasting change into the world by means of the gospel of Jesus Christ. You need to share with the people whom only you can reach. You must communicate how God has shown His great love for them in Jesus.

We need to change this world from the inside out, and only the gospel of Jesus Christ has the power to do that. But until you and I make it a part of our everyday lives to reach out with that message, all talk about changing the world, making it a better and more joyful place to live, will be just so many empty words. There will be no changed world without changed people. And there will be no truly changed people if they have not been changed from the inside out. And there will be no such changes without the continuous, bold, believing sharing of the gospel of Jesus Christ on the part of each and every one of us who is determined to change our world now.

The challenge is great, and the path is fraught with difficulty. But the results to be achieved in terms of changed lives are more than worth the effort. We must stay ever mindful of what the Irish poet William Butler Yeats said in his poem, "Adam's Curse":

> "I said: 'It's certain there is no fine thing
> Since Adam's fall but needs much labouring.' "

If not us, who? If not now, when?

We hold the answers to those questions within us. Let us determine to be the generation that captured the moment and took the initiative to change the world—from the inside out!

Questions for Study or Discussion

1. Jesus gave us the Holy Spirit to provide us with power. According to Acts 1:8, what was that power supposed to do in us?

2. What would you say are some of the primary obstacles keeping Christian people from sharing the gospel with others?

3. Make a list of the first names of everyone you know who needs to hear the gospel. Now claim God's promise of Acts 1:8 to use you to share with them.

For Further Reading

Conn, Harvie M. *Evangelism: Doing Justice and Preaching Grace.* Grand Rapids, Mich.: Zondervan, 1982.

Kennedy, D. James. *Evangelism Explosion.* Wheaton, Ill.: Tyndale House, 1983.

Moore, T. M. *Witnesses Unto Me.* Evangelism Explosion, P.O. Box 23820, Fort Lauderdale, FL 33307.

4

No Final Obstacle

A Lesson from History

It is a principle of military strategy as old as warfare itself, and the powerful Macedonian king knew it well: Strike down the leader and you subdue the army. From the moment he crossed the Bosporus and set foot on the plains of ancient Troy, Alexander the Great, king of Macedonia and self-proclaimed "avenger of the Greeks," knew that the surest way to victory in his campaign against the Persians would be to kill Darius III in battle. Hopefully, that triumph would come by his own hand.

Carefully Alexander laid the groundwork for his final thrust into Persia, subduing lesser peoples and securing the coastal cities in Asia so as to preclude the Persians' being resupplied from either the provinces or the sea. At last, convinced that all was in readiness, he set his eyes toward Persepolis and began the grand advance against the Persian monarch.

After a march which lasted throughout the summer of 331 B.C., Alexander arrived with 47,000 troops to face over a million Persians[1] and Indians under the leadership of Darius at Gaugamela in what is now Iran.

The battle began almost like a ballet, with the highly organized Greeks advancing, dispersing, and regrouping as one, in order to deceive their more numerous foes, ever looking for a point of weakness in the lines. As the battle became pitched, dust filling the air and the cries of men and the shrieks of horses piercing through the clash of iron and flesh, a sudden opportunity presented itself to Alexander. Through a combination of precisely timed and perfectly executed moves by his outer flanks, Alexander was able to create a sense of disorder in the center of the Persian horde. All at once, for an instant, there was exposed to his view the golden chariot of Darius. With a great cry and a bold surge, Alexander led 2,000 of his companions into the gap, hurling his own spear at the Persian king, only to see it strike his charioteer a fatal blow. Darius, confused, startled, and at last terrified to see his foe pressing down upon him, turned and fled with 10,000 men, leaving over a million warriors to an uncertain fate.

Darius fled to Afghanistan, then to the Caspian Sea, and finally, to Khavar in the heart of Persia. There Alexander, with only sixty horsemen, overtook Darius at last, only to find that he had been killed by his own courtiers.

His most loyal followers knew that the defeat of Darius III at Gaugamela had been final. The army of a million men was scattered and destroyed. After Gaugamela the great cities of the mighty Persian Empire fell to Alexander one by one, with scarcely a struggle—mighty Babylon, powerful Susa, splendid Persepolis, all became the possessions of the victorious Macedonian. The defeat of Darius at Gaugamela infused a spirit of inevitable triumph into the Greek army. They knew that there remained no final obstacle to their dream of world dominance.

In just such a way Christians must see that there is no final obstacle in the way of their moving ahead with confidence to change the world through the love of Jesus Christ. The final enemy has been destroyed. The arch-rival has been vanquished. His ultimate weapon has been rendered utterly ineffectual. And nothing stands between us and the fullness of Christ's blessings except our own lack of initiative and resolve.

The Significance of the Cross

The great work that Jesus Christ accomplished for us on the cross is significant for many reasons. Not the least of these is the fact that on the cross He overwhelmingly defeated those who would use us in their demonic schemes to make a mockery of the glory of God. As the apostle Paul puts it:

And you, being dead in your sins and the uncircumcision of your flesh, hath he quickened together with him, having forgiven you all trespasses; Blotting out the handwriting of ordinances that was against us, which was contrary to us, and took it out of the way, nailing it to his cross; And having spoiled principalities and powers, he made a shew of them openly, triumphing over them in it.

Colossians 2:13–15

On the cross Jesus Christ crushed the head of Satan (Gen. 3:15), thereby guaranteeing that he should no more have power over us to keep us from realizing all the goodness and blessedness of God. Furthermore, His resurrection from the dead is our guarantee that not even death itself is an obstacle to halt at, a final terror to keep us from serving our Lord. There is coming a day, says Paul, in which we will mock death, berating its futile attempts to keep us from the eternal glory of God (1 Cor. 15:54–57). This being so, we need have no present fear of even this most frightening of human prospects, for, as Paul has said, "For me to live is Christ, *and to die is gain*" (Phil. 1:21, italics added).

Thus, since the one who would rob us of the joy and power of our salvation has been sent scurrying away in shame from the cross of Christ, crushed and defeated and without power over our lives, even the greatest of our fears has been overcome by the death and resurrection of our Lord. There remains *no final obstacle* to our moving ahead at once to claim the heritage of promises and blessings that is ours to possess in this life and throughout the ages of eternity.

There is no final obstacle to our moving ahead to change the world in the name of Jesus Christ! We are told that God, who has so graciously given us His only begotten Son, will with Christ "freely give us all things" (Rom. 8:32).

Obstacles in Our Path

Yet many believers today seem hardly convinced of these great truths. Our lethargy and reticence bear stark testimony to our lack of comprehension concerning the victory that Christ has gained for us. It is as though He had never defeated the devil, never overcome the terror of death, never poured out His Spirit in power among us. We firmly believe that the simple reason today's Christians are not the world changers Christ intends them to be is that they do not fully grasp the magnitude of His victory on the cross and in the empty tomb. Thus, they are neither challenged nor emboldened to believe Him for the great things He has promised to do for us (Jer. 33:3). Our path to final victory seems blocked by obstacles at every turn.

What hindrances stand in the way of our changing the world? How has Jesus Christ nullified their power over our lives? And, most importantly, how can we begin to realize victory in every aspect of our lives?

We believe that there are four primary obstacles to our changing the world. If we could come to understand these impediments from the perspective of Christ's victory on the cross, we would be able to move ahead in becoming true world changers. Christ's death and resurrection have nullified the work of Satan. He has been once and for all defeated by our Savior and Lord. Since this is true, there is no need for us to allow any lesser blockades to stand in the way of our realizing all that we have been promised in the gospel.

The first of these apparent obstacles is the inability to believe that God could do anything significant through us as individuals. The vast majority of Christians have an inexcusably bad self-image. Many would hardly dare believe that God could win others to Christ through them—that He could work through them to demonstrate His love and compassion in a powerful and influential way and could use them to take a significant public stand for some matter of truth or morality. In their own eyes these Christians are little nobodies, running around in a world that needs great big somebodies to make it better. They cannot bring themselves to believe that anything they might do could contribute to changing the world.

We must come to see that this obstacle to our ever getting started as effective world changers for Christ has been rendered invalid by His work on the cross. Jesus died at Calvary to bring reconciliation to a people who would believe on Him and find peace with God. The apostle Paul puts it this way:

> And, having made peace through the blood of his cross, by him to reconcile all things unto himself; by him, I say, whether they be things in earth, or things in heaven. And you, that were sometime

alienated and enemies in your mind by wicked works, yet now hath
he reconciled In the body of his flesh through death, to present you
holy and unblameable and unreprovable in his sight.

Colossians 1:20–22, italics added

In other words, as God looks upon those of us who have
received the gift of eternal life through the finished work of Jesus
Christ, He sees us as *lacking nothing we require* to live the life of
good works He has prepared for us (Eph. 2:10). Our standing in
His eyes is *perfect,* and we are ready to get on with the task of
passing around His reconciliation to others. And notice that
*there is no distinction drawn in this passage between believers of
any kind.* We stand all alike before the approving, loving eye of
our heavenly Father, lacking nothing we might need to serve
Him as we ought. As Paul says later in that same Epistle, "And
ye are complete in Him" (Col. 2:10). No matter who you are or
what your position in life—*complete* in Him. No matter how low
your opinion of your abilities might be—*complete* in Him. No
matter how many times you have said to yourself that God
simply could not do anything through you—*complete* in Him.

No wonder Jesus said that we are the salt of the earth and the
light of the world! No wonder Peter refers to us as a royal priest-
hood, a chosen generation, a people who can show forth the
praises of God! There is no reason for thinking that we could
never be used in significant ways to change the world. Jesus'
death on the cross and His resurrection from the grave are the
guarantee for us that we stand approved and complete before
the throne of our Father, fully equipped in Him to serve as He
leads in this world.

Someone may protest that he has no power of speech with
which to declare his faith. Jesus has promised to provide the
words we need (Luke 12:11–12). Another may lament her lack
of resources to give toward the world-changing work of Christ.
God will supply all we need through Him (Phil. 4:19). Or you
may feel that you simply have no special talent to contribute
toward making this a better world. Have you not seen that the
crucified and risen Christ has given you gifts and abilities you
have yet to discover (Eph. 4:7–10)? We are complete in Him,
approved by God for the work to which we have been called in
this day!

A poor self-image is not a justifiable reason for our failure to become the world changers we have been created in Christ Jesus to be.

The second apparent obstacle that can keep us from moving out to change the world is nothing more than a simple lack of obedience to the teachings and principles of our Lord. How many in the Christian community know what they should be doing, but simply choose not to obey the clear teaching of God's Word? They see the Scriptures as instructing them to love their neighbors as themselves, but are unimaginative and delinquent in fulfilling that command. They know that the Bible summons them to be witnesses to Christ, but they simply fail each time they are presented with the opportunity to tell someone about the Lord. They know that there is unconfessed sin in their lives, sin which keeps them from becoming the world changers they have been called to be, yet they often fail to repent. This lack of obedience to the clear teaching of the Scriptures, as powerful as it is in keeping us inactive in the faith, is merely an apparent obstacle to our becoming true world changers. For, by His death and resurrection, Jesus has overcome even the grip of disobedience in our lives.

What causes disobedience? There are many reasons, but one of the most common is a simple lack of trust. Many believers just fail to have the necessary faith in God and His Word that they should have when "push comes to shove" in their lives. They do not witness because they simply are not fully convinced witnessing is really important or that the gospel is really something everyone needs. What I mean is, *they do not trust that God knows best* when He tells us to preach the gospel to every creature. So, many act on feelings and fears instead of His truth and hide their light under a bushel. Since many fail to trust the example of Christ and the trustworthiness of His teaching, they attend mainly to their own needs and concerns and let the rest of humanity fend for itself. *If we could but trust Him more completely, we would be able to love more perfectly.* We fail to take the moral stands that we should because we do not trust that God's way is better and more urgent than what *we* might choose. Thus, our impulses and fears often determine our conduct more than our faith in God's Word.

Yet, what the cross and the empty tomb show us is quite

another story. The cross declares the urgency of the gospel for our day. Only the cross can erase human sin and divert a lost soul from the pathway of destruction to that of life. The empty tomb is God's guarantee that the cross is significant and the *only* effective means to gain life. When we come to see Christ's work in a more perfect light, witnessing for Him will begin to take on a new importance. We soon come to see that unless His death and resurrection are personally appropriated by the men and women whom we meet each day, *they will perish in their sins.* And it might well be that *unless we take the time to tell them*— unless we trust God that this message is absolutely crucial to their eternal well-being and reach out to them in faith—they may never hear and have the opportunity to come to salvation in Christ. We must learn to trust God that His gospel is the *sine qua non* for human happiness and well-being. When we do, we will not fail to tell others about the Good News of Christ.

Likewise, we must see the cross as the supreme example of the power of love. "For God so loved the world . . . ." We know the words well, yet have we truly considered that it was Jesus' love for each of us that compelled Him to endure the cross, despising the shame, so that we might find life in Him? His love for us gave Him the power to endure, which has resulted in our having eternal life! When we come to see the magnitude of God's love for us, when we truly come to understand it in a personal and powerful way, we will be driven to love others in the day-to-day affairs of our lives. "We love . . ." wrote the apostle John, "because he first loved us" (1 John 4:19).

As we come to understand the incredible drawing power of God's love in our lives, we will be able to trust Him to make that power effectual in our relationships with others. *We will not fear to love, but will trust God to empower us and to use our love for others to point them more clearly to Him.*

In the same way, we can learn to trust God for the moral strength and courage required in these days. Sin hanged Jesus on the cross. It was sin's pain and suffering He was forced to endure. He diverted sin's penalty onto Himself and away from us. It was to put away sin once and for all that He rose from the grave as the victor over the very author of iniquity. Our ability to walk in the path of righteousness and to stand for biblical morality derives from our trusting Christ, who has overcome sin and pointed the way to a fuller, more meaningful life. As we look to Him on the cross and risen from the dead, we find the strength we need to be the kind of moral individuals we have been born again to be in Christ. Our beloved Savior's death on the cross can lead us to hate sin, and His resurrection can empower us to overcome it.

The apostle James said, "Therefore to him that knoweth to do good, and doeth it not, to him it is sin" (James 4:17). By coming to understand more fully the work of Christ on the cross and the meaning of His resurrection from the dead, we can develop the trust in God we need to keep this sin of disobedience from taking control of our lives and preventing us from becoming world changers.

The third apparent obstacle to our becoming effective world changers is nothing more than a simple lack of time. How can we possibly fulfill all our responsibilities and still have time left over to get involved in activities we hope will change the world? There are not enough hours in the day for what we have to do already. How can we make time for anything more?

The problem of "too little time" is really a problem of confused priorities. Someone once asked a new Christian if he had started reading his Bible yet. The new believer replied that he had not, but that he really wanted to begin soon. His friend said, "No, you don't." The new Christian was astonished! What did he mean, "No, you don't"? What real Christian did not want to read his Bible each day? He just had not been able to make the time for it yet.

But that wise Christian pointed out something that none of us should ever forget: We will do in our lives only and exactly what we really want to do, and nothing more. That is, we make time for the things that we perceive to be most important. Our lives are a hodgepodge of priorities, and not all of them are consistent with our new life in Christ. As we come to see His death and resurrection in a clearer light, we will want to rearrange our priorities accordingly, and then we will begin to become the world changers He wants us to be.

Jesus Christ came to earth to do the work of His Father, to bring fullness and peace to men so that they might know God and walk in His ways. But, to accomplish this, Jesus Himself had to establish certain priorities for His life and ministry. Thus, it was inevitable that from time to time He would disappoint the people around Him because what they wanted Him to do did not fit the total agenda He had established for Himself. He could not preach in every town. He could not see to the healing of every sick or lame person. He could not bring a word of comfort or hope to all who needed it. But what *could* Jesus do?

He and He alone could die on the cross for us. And, regardless of the fact that there was so much to do, despite His awareness of this most difficult task of all, and mindful of the pleas of Peter and the rest that He should take some more "reasonable" course, Jesus kept His priorities straight and fulfilled the work the Father had given Him.

This is what He calls us to do as well. "But seek ye first the kingdom of God . . ." (Matt. 6:33). Let us examine our priorities in the light of the saving work of Jesus Christ. How many of us begin each day asking God to show us what we must do that day to help establish the kingdom of Christ more firmly in our own lives and in our world? Do we really "walk circumspectly . . . redeeming the time," as Paul suggests (Eph. 5:15–16), or do we simply bounce along through life like pinballs, propelled by whatever the world and our circumstances bring our way?

The cross and the empty tomb ought to convince us that God will honor the keeping of His priorities in our lives. We must become more diligent about setting priorities for our daily lives that follow in the historical stream of what Christ was working to accomplish on the cross. If we can use His example to guide us in our planning and in the choice of activities we make for our lives, we can become the world changers that He died and rose again to enable us to become.

The final apparent obstacle that gets in the way of our becoming true world changers is the fear of men. Because we are afraid of what others might think, we do not witness, we do not reach out in love, we do not take personal and public moral stands. We are afraid of being laughed at, mocked, rejected, or disliked. Since we do not want to offend anyone, we often withhold from others the only word or the only deed that might show them what the truth and love of God are really like.

The Lord observed this tendency among His people in the Old Testament, and He had some things to say about it:

I, even I, am he that comforteth you: who art thou, that thou shouldest be afraid of a man that shall die, and of the son of man which shall be made as grass; And forgettest the LORD thy maker, that hath stretched forth the heavens, and laid the foundations of the earth; and hast feared continually every day because of the fury of the oppressor, as if he were ready to destroy? and where is the fury of the oppressor? The captive exile hasteneth that he may be loosed, and that he should not die in the pit, nor that his bread should fail. But I am the LORD thy God, that 'vided the sea, whose waves roared: The LORD of hosts is his name. And I have put my words in thy mouth, and I have covered thee in the shadow of mine hand, that I may plant the heavens, and lay the foundations of the earth, and say unto Zion, Thou art my people.

Isaiah 51:12–16

The cross and empty tomb can enable us to look beyond our fear of men to the glories that await us in the service of God's kingdom. Do men seek to deride and discomfort us? The risen Christ has sent His Comforter to live in our hearts. He can encourage and console us as no human comforter could ever do. Do others seek to do us harm because of our stances on issues of morality? Christ has borne each blow for us a hundred times over. His strength can enable us to withstand the pain. Would men follow the captain of sin into battle against the people of Christ, to injure or despise them? Let us take comfort and encouragement in knowing that they serve a defeated and crushed monarch who has no power over us.

We can overcome the fear of what others might think or do by fixing our eyes on Jesus and drawing on His strength to help us become the world changers He wants us to be. The blessings are there for those who overcome the obstacles to changing the world, who know that there is really no final obstacle to our achieving the victory, and who reach out, speak up, and stand firm to show forth the glory of God and the cause of Christ to a lost and dying generation.

No Final Obstacle

Brothers and sisters in Christ, if we are to become the generation that changes the world, we must look beyond these apparent obstacles to the final triumph achieved on Calvary and out of the garden tomb. No poor self-image, no lack of trust, no want of time, and no fear of men can stand in the way of those who know that their victory has been perfectly secured by their invincible Lord and King. We have only to begin to witness, to reach out in love to others, and to insist on decency and biblical morality at every turn to see the power of the risen Savior begin to overcome the apparent obstacles in our lives.

As Alexander returned from Khavar with the news of Darius' death, what do you suppose the response of his troops must have been? Did they begin packing their gear for the return to Greece? Did they leisurely resort to planting the battle-scarred earth for next season's harvest? Did they fall to moaning and complaining over the battles yet to come? Did they dispense themselves to the hundred and one activities that men can find to divert them from the crucial issues at hand?

No! To a man, the cry went up, loud, long, and filled with the prospect of great victory: "On to Babylon! On to Susa! On to Persepolis!"

There was no final obstacle. The spoils of their commander's glorious victory lay ready for the taking. And the warriors of their great king were eager to resume the challenge.

How is it among the warriors of the still greater King, the very King of Kings Himself? Have we come to see that there is no final obstacle in the way of our changing the world for the glory of our Master?

Notes

1. Robin Lane Fox, *Alexander the Great* (New York: The Dial Press, 1973), p. 229.

Questions for Study or Discussion

1. Let's look at each of the four obstacles to becoming an effective world changer:

- Do you really believe God could use you in some significant way for His world-changing purposes? List some areas in which you might be available to God.
- Are there any areas of disobedience in your life? Would you be willing to confess them and leave them behind?

- Are there any activities that you could forsake in order to become a more effective world changer?
- Are you afraid of men? In what way? What they might think? Say? Do? Can you let God be sufficient to overcome your fears?

2. How would you describe Paul's resolve to be an effective world changer as he conveys it in Philippians 3:12–14?

For Further Reading

Colson, Charles. *Loving God.* Grand Rapids, Mich.: Zondervan, 1983.

Schaeffer, Francis A. *True Spirituality.* Wheaton, Ill.: Tyndale House, 1971.

5

Remodeling Your Home

What's in a Home?

In recent years, with interest rates still high and a scarcity of jobs keeping mobility at a minimum, there has developed a great deal of interest in home maintenance and remodeling. Rather than move to a newer, larger home, many couples have taken to adding on a room, putting in new carpeting, or refurnishing their homes. Remodeling has become the latest craze, which, it is hoped, will bring a sense of renewal to homes that have become cramped, shabby, or stale.

But can we expect mere physical remodeling of the structure or furnishings of a home to relieve the tremendous pressures and problems mounting on all sides and threatening to destroy the traditional family? A home is more than four walls, plush carpets, or distinctive furnishings. A home is people, and in our day the people who inhabit the homes of America have been plunged into bewilderment over the breakup of families they have known and loved for many years. They wonder, "How could this have happened? Could it happen to us? What can we do to prevent it?"

Clearly, the homes of our land are in need of some drastic remodeling, but remodeling of a sort which goes beyond the mere cosmetic changes that have held and dissipated the hopes of increasing numbers of broken families in recent months and years. The reconditioning that today's families require must reach to the very depths of the persons who live together under the same roof. If the homes of America are to become once again the proving ground for the next generation of America's and the world's greatest leaders, they must undergo deep and abiding change, which can come only from trusting in God.

Thus, the world changers of our day must address themselves to the family's need for remodeling and change. And the key to this whole matter lies with today's Christian parents.

Not long ago an athletic-awards banquet was held at a large high school in the Midwest. As the coach was introducing the players and handing out the letters indicating their individual achievements, it was apparent that he took great pride in each one. He had a sincere compliment for each player and was careful to note that one's unique contribution to the team's season.

At the end of the ceremony only one letter remained to be presented. The coach had left the captain's award for last, and for a reason that was apparent to all.

This young man was not only the captain of the team, but he was also its outstanding player and one of the top students in his class. All who knew him agreed that he was an upright and friendly fellow, one who could be trusted and who was not afraid of responsibility. As the coach introduced him, he made a comment that many of those present would not soon forget: "I can think of no finer thing to say about this last young man than that I wish he were my son."

Of course, what the coach was saying was that he hoped his own young son would grow up to be as fine an example as the captain of his football team was for all his peers. Everyone present on that evening knew that the character of the young man had been carefully nurtured in a home where decency, love, hard work, responsibility, and duty were among the virtues constantly extolled and modeled by his parents. In many ways this young man was nothing more than the projection into a new generation of the values, commitments, determination, and example of his parents. They were in large part the reason that he was the kind of person whom all held in admiration and respect.

The Example of Jesus

If there was ever a person whom we might wish our children to take as an example for their lives, certainly it would be Jesus

of Nazareth. Jesus has been recognized down through the ages
as the supreme example of goodness and truth. Faithful parents
of many generations have prayed that their children might become more like Jesus each day. The future of this world would
be much brighter by far if each Christian home could be reasonably assured that the children nurtured there would follow in the
steps of Jesus all the days of their lives.

It was said of Jesus as a young man that He grew "in wisdom
and stature, and in favour with God and man" (Luke 2:52). As
the days in Nazareth went by and Jesus advanced in years, He
gained increasing amounts of the godly wisdom that would give
Him the skill to live according to the will of God in the whole of
His life. As He grew closer to God and to understanding and
accepting God's plan for Him, Jesus learned to love men and
found that they loved Him in return. He became the epitome of
all that God required in the One who would accomplish the
salvation of His people through His perfect life, loving sacrifice
on the cross, and powerful resurrection from the dead.

But notice something about how this was accomplished. Luke
tells us that during those years in which He was becoming fitted
for His great work, Jesus went to Nazareth to live with His
parents "and was subject unto them" (Luke 2:51).

For some thirty years, Jesus of Nazareth subjected Himself to
the character, influence, and guidance of Joseph and Mary. Just
as God would use John the Baptist to prepare the way of the
Messiah, He used Mary and Joseph to prepare the Messiah for
His way. And I believe that if we can gain some clearer insights
into the kind of people these two were and the types of models
they provided for the young Savior, we might be able to discover
something of the wisdom we need for remodeling our homes
according to the will and purpose of God.

Joseph

Of Joseph, not much is said in the Word of God. Yet what is
said holds worlds of insight for us into the nature of this myste-
rious and blessed man.

In the first place, we might note of Joseph that he was most
certainly a humble man. He was the son of David, the heir to the
throne of Israel! Yet, we see in Joseph no grasping after David's

crown, no resentment of the Romans who were keeping him from his throne, no bitterness at being reduced to a humble station in the midst of an ordinary village far from the glories of Jerusalem (Matt. 1:6-16). There was no querulousness about this man; he accepted his lot in life with humility, knowing it to have been given to him by the Lord. Doubtless such humility and submission to the will of God would have made a deep impression on the children who inhabited his home, including the One who, in His resignation to God's will, became the hope of the world.

Second, we are told that Joseph was a just man (Matt. 1:19). That is, he had a zeal for the law of God, knowing it to be the foundation of a just society. Thus, when Mary was discovered to be pregnant before their marriage had been consummated, Joseph first sought to follow the spirit of the law and have her put away. Since only the Romans could have carried out the punishment required by Mosaic Law (Deut. 22:22-24), Joseph sought annulment as the next most prudent thing within his power. His concern for the keeping of God's law outweighed even his emotional ties to the woman to whom he was betrothed, although it is obvious that he loved her dearly. To Joseph, the justice of God was far more important than the satisfaction of personal desires.

Notice also that Joseph was not hasty in judgment. He thought on this matter long and hard before he decided what it was he must do (Matt. 1:20). Many today are given to actions motivated by impulse or mere emotion. Not so this humble carpenter. He gave careful thought and doubtless much prayerful consideration to the meaning of his circumstances in the light of what he knew to be the law of God before he put his decisions into action.

In this also is revealed the tenderness and consideration of Joseph toward Mary. He was not willing to embarrass or shame her publicly (Matt. 1:19). Undoubtedly this tenderness would show through time and again for the children of that household to see and experience. He who so tenderly spoke such words as "Talitha cumi" (Mark 5:41), no doubt learned such gentleness in part from the man who was head of the home in which He spent His childhood.

We also find in Joseph a willingness to fulfill the will of God for his life. He did not hesitate to obey the words revealed to him by the angel concerning Mary and her condition (Matt. 1:20-24). Moreover, after the birth of Jesus, Joseph can be seen leading his family to Jerusalem to fulfill the requirements of the law (Luke 2:21-24; cf. Exod. 13:2). We are told further that Joseph took his family to Jerusalem every year to observe the Passover (Luke 2:41). This most sacred feast, which marked the deliverance of God's people from their captivity in Egypt, doubtless had special meaning for Joseph as he watched Jesus adhering to the rituals that His own life would supplant in later years.

Joseph was also an honorable man. In Matthew 1:25 we are told that he refrained from sexual intimacy with Mary until after Jesus was born. Knowing what he did about the Holy Child in Mary's womb (Matt. 1:20-21), Joseph may have wanted to protect the divine plan by making certain it would be known by all that he was most certainly not the father of Jesus. And he was willing to endure whatever scorn or opprobrium might have been directed toward him, for the sake of what he knew to be God's plan.

We see Joseph also as a hard-working and productive man, a master carpenter. It is a matter of no small significance that years later, after Jesus had begun His ministry, Joseph was remembered in death not by name, but by the trade for which all had come to esteem him. Jesus was "the carpenter's son" (Matt. 13:55), or so it was supposed. Just as we might say, in trying to remember some great person of days gone by, "Who was that great king who did thus and so? Or that great composer who wrote such and such?" so Joseph was remembered by the trade he had no doubt mastered in the city that could not abide the One who had been nurtured within his home.

Joseph's concern for his children and their future is perhaps best seen in his having taught Jesus the trade that he had come to know so well. Jesus was known as a carpenter after the fashion of his father, as Joseph was supposed to have been (Mark 6:3). What patience, what love, and what skill must have been required to instruct those young children in the tasks they would need to master in order to survive and prosper.

Finally, we see Joseph as an extremely resourceful man. He was not one to look for a handout or to bemoan his circumstances, be they ever so adverse. Joseph was able to provide for his family in whatever situation they found themselves. Thus, he was able to secure and maintain a house during their stay in Bethlehem (Matt. 2:11). And, in another country among people whose ways they did not know, Joseph was nevertheless able to see to it that all their needs were met (Matt. 2:14–23). Whatever the situation, Joseph had a way of knowing what had to be done and of making sure that it was taken care of. Thus, he was used of God to provide a safe and secure home for the Son who would become the Savior of the world.

Mary

Of the virtues of Mary, we are perhaps somewhat more aware. Mary and Joseph would have had at least an equal influence on Jesus during His formative years in Nazareth.

From the same family line as Joseph, Mary had learned as well the joys of the humble life. We find in her no vain pining for the life of a princess. We see also in her the same receptivity to the Word of God as in her husband. When the angel came to announce her election by God to bear His Son, she proved a willing vessel for His purposes (Luke 1:29, 34, 38). Here was a woman who, despite the public suspicion that she would have to endure for the sake of God's will, nonetheless rejoiced to have the will of God fulfilled in her life.

Mary also reveals a gracious and artistic bent in her song of praise to the Lord for His salvation to His people (Luke 1:46–55). Although from a village in the country, Mary was not unacquainted with the beauties of poetry and song. Moreover, in the song given her by the Lord, she showed herself to be thankful and contented in the will of God and well aware of His larger purposes for those who would trust in Him. Matters of theology and faith were not foreign to her understanding. Could it be that Jesus, who had such regard for sparrows, flowers in the field, and every jot and tittle of God's law, could have learned from this godly woman some of what He took into His ministry?

Mary is also seen to be a thoughtful, reflective woman. There is nothing scatterbrained or flippant about her. Matters affecting her life and the lives of those she loved were given the most serious consideration in her quiet moments (Luke 2:19, 51).

She is seen to have the same regard as her husband for the rituals and practices of their faith. Mary was no obstacle for Joseph in his attempt to build a godly home. Indeed, she was as much a force for godliness as her husband to this end.

Finally, Mary reveals a loving and concerned heart, especially as this touches those who are close to her. In Luke 1:48 we see her much distraught over her missing child, grieved and concerned over Jesus' absence and sorrowful at the distress she obviously saw in her husband. And she remained the loving mother to the very end, weeping at the crucified feet of her Son as He bore the sins of the world (John 19:25–26).

Thus, Jesus spent His early years in a home where love, devotion, faith, responsibility, hard work, care, consideration, and honor were the daily fare, modeled and taught by parents whose love for God motivated all they did. In the hands of Joseph and Mary, His heavenly Father had found two who could be trusted to provide the environment, attention, and training that Jesus would require in order to prepare Him for His great work.

We would do well to consider how our homes might be remodeled according to the example of Joseph and Mary. If our children are to grow up to acquire something of the character of the Lord Jesus Christ, we must make every effort as Christian parents to provide a setting in which the virtues of His life-style are exemplified, discussed, and extolled. Only thus will our children come to esteem a life-style that is truly world changing in its impact. And only thus will our homes be able to survive the onslaught of turmoil, which has arisen and is being experienced by so many in our day.

The Challenge to Christian Parents

What, then, can Christian parents do to remodel their homes after the pattern established by Joseph and Mary?

First, let us concentrate on providing a model that our children can emulate. As Christian parents, we must be diligent to get our own lives in order before the Lord so that our children will have constantly before them the examples of love, patience, virtue, faith, and responsibility that we want them to acquire. Only as Christian parents work at growing in their own relationships with the Lord Jesus Christ will they be able realistically to

expect the same from their children. Let us work to lay aside the
sins so common among those in the world—greed, materialism,
lust, sluggardliness, self-concern—and let us cultivate life-styles
that enable us to exemplify the life of Christ and to reach out in
His name to others, beginning with our children.

As we grow and become more excited about the life we have
in God, our children will be more inclined to emulate that which
they see in us. We must be diligent, and we must be genuine.
Unless we are studying to become all that we can be in Christ,
we are unrealistic and unfair to expect the same of our children.

Second, we must help our children to see the sovereignty of
God in all its breadth and depth. We must show them that His
overarching care for them extends even to their most mundane
and intimate concerns. Jesus had learned that His heavenly Father was as concerned for falling sparrows and the hairs on our
heads as for the rain that falls on the just and unjust alike. We
must help our children to see that God's concern extends to the
totality of their own lives and to the whole of humanity in the
world. There is nothing too small for them to take to Him in
prayer, nothing too great for Him to handle, nothing too mundane to be beyond the pale of His concern, nothing too terrible
for Him to know about and forgive. Our children will truly come
to understand and rest in God's sovereignty only as we help
them think about it in all its greatness and beauty.

Third, we must help our children develop a deep sense of
responsibility for the lives of others and the purposes of God in
the world. We must help them see from the beginning that whatever they may choose to do in life, their lives belong to God for
His purposes. They must be taught and encouraged to take upon
themselves the burden of Christ's Great Commission. They must
be led to see their work in the light of God's will for them and
for His world. They must see that our work for the Lord goes far
beyond the mere constraints of our particular job, whatever that
job may be. And they must be helped to develop the burden for
others that was characteristic of the Lord during His earthly
sojourn.

Our children are the world changers of the future, and unless
we begin to teach them to have an outlook of responsibility for
the things of God in the world, we cannot expect that they will
be able to succeed in their generation.

Fourth, we must be careful not to minimize the affairs pertaining to our faith. In our personal lives and in what we expect of our children we must show the importance of such things as witnessing for Christ, studying the Word of God, prayer, the local church, missions, the tithe, and so forth. Our children will not automatically learn that these matters are of importance. It is up to us to exemplify and teach them.

Fifth, we must cultivate in our children those traits conducive to well-rounded character. We must help them become alert, observant, and creative. As we teach them the beauties of music, literature, and art, we must help them see how each of these and all the wonders of the world around us redound each day to the glory of our magnificent God. And we must encourage them to make their own personal contributions in these areas as they are led of their heavenly Father. Each child's drawing and every piano recital and school program can be an opportunity for Christian parents to help their children see how these and a hundred other areas of their lives can bring praise to God in the here and now.

Finally, we must help our children to see the beauty and importance of a Christian home. We must be willing to talk to them in love about matters of intimate concern for their lives and to encourage them to look forward to a day when they will have children of their own. We must be ready to enter into their experiences and help them feel as much a part of the family and home as we feel ourselves to be. And we must be careful to protect them from the evils of our society—on television, in the press, and in our communities—that threaten not only the stability of the home but our entire society as well.

We must give ourselves without reservation to the task of building Christian homes, loving homes like the one in which Jesus was reared, homes where the virtues and blessings of life with God are both demonstrated and inculcated. It is up to the Christian parents of this generation to begin. We cannot change the world for Jesus Christ if we are too busy outside our homes to give our children the attention they need. Let us each one consider what his or her task may be in contributing to the creation of the next generation of world changers for Jesus Christ.

Arrows into the Future

In Psalm 127 children are likened unto arrows in the hand of a mighty warrior. What an appropriate way of thinking about the generation to follow after us! A mighty warrior is a strong force to reckon with. But with a bow and arrows he becomes even more potent, for the arrows can accomplish his aims at a distance far removed from him. It is not necessary for the warrior to be present for his arrows to have their powerful effect.

Long after we have gone, our children and their children will still be in the world, living out in their experience the lessons they learned in our homes. What sort of arrows will we send into the future? Will our children be true world changers, or will they be pressed into the world's mold, unable or unwilling to resist its pressure and allure?

In large part the answer to that question is in the hands of the Christian parents of today. Let us resolve to remodel our homes in such a way that the arrows we launch into the next generation will accomplish the world-changing purposes so important to us and to our Lord today.

Questions for Study or Discussion

1. Take a moment to analyze the time you currently spend with your children. When is it? How much is it? Of what does it consist?

2. Make a list of the primary character traits you want your children to acquire. What can you do to help ensure that these become a reality in your children?

3. Are there any negative influences in your home that might be interfering with the character development of your children?

For Further Reading

Crabb, Jr., Lawrence J. *The Marriage Builder.* Grand Rapids, Mich.: Zondervan, 1982.

Dobson, James. *Hide or Seek.* Old Tappan, N.J.: Fleming H. Revell, 1974.

Schaeffer, Edith. *What Is a Family?* Old Tappan, N.J.: Fleming H. Revell, 1975.

6

Economics for a Changed World

The Mystery of Economics

Economics.

Just say the word and, for most of us, visions of obscure, far-off concepts and institutions begin to rise and fall in our minds. Supply-side, fiscal policy, IMF, demand curve, GNP, leading indicators, consumer price index, inflation, stagflation, M1, M2, M3. . . .

Is it any wonder that most Americans, and certainly most Christians, view economics as merely some abstract and imperfect set of principles describing and prescribing something to do with our national and personal wealth—but who knows what?

And economists, who can understand them? Apart from Karl Marx and Adam Smith, who among us can even name an important member of that genus?

Which just serves to highlight the problem. *For certainly it was never in the plan of God that His people should be ignorant or indifferent concerning matters of economic interest.* How can we change the world if we remain uninformed about the resources of men and nations? The answer is that we cannot. If we are to change the world, we must take seriously the economic responsibilities that have been laid upon us.

We must each accept the duty and challenge of striving after a biblical system of economics that can change the world.

The fact is that each and every one of us is an economist.

There is no way around it. The word *economics* comes from the Greek *oikonomia*, which suggests the management of a household, overseeing of all the tasks, responsibilities, and resources associated with a home and possessions. Economics at its most basic is simply the systematic study of how people manage their resources and opportunities. The apostle Paul says that every man should think of us as stewards of the mysteries and blessings of God with which we have been entrusted (1 Cor. 4:1). Literally translated, Paul says, "Let people consider us as God's economists [*oikonomous*]."

The question, therefore, is not whether or not we shall be concerned about economics. The question is whether we are to be conscious or unconscious, good or bad, or—to use Jesus' terms—profitable or unprofitable economists of God.

And in this age, when there is so much competition for our energies, resources, and time, we cannot afford the luxury of a merely cavalier attitude toward this critical question. If the kingdom of God is to go forth in power, capturing every thought for Jesus Christ, converting men in the whole of their lives for the gospel, and receiving an ever-increasing utilization of the time and resources of human beings for divine purposes, we who are God's economists must give serious consideration to the requirement laid down for us in this area. In effect Paul says, "It is required of God's economists that they be found faithful" (1 Cor. 4:2).

Faithfulness on the part of God's people is the only way to assert the economic outlook and behavior that can change the world.

Profitable and Unprofitable Economics

In Matthew 25:14–30, Jesus presents a parable that can give us some insight into the characteristics of profitable and unprofitable managers of goods and services. In this story three servants are entrusted with varying amounts of a master's financial resources, with the understanding that they will put them to good use while the master is away. At the end of the story only two of the servants are found to be profitable. By focusing on the unprofitable servant, we can get a glimpse into what is required of us if we are to be God's profitable economists.

Notice that the unprofitable servant is held accountable for two things. First of all (v. 26), he is accountable for failing to know what was expected of him as a servant of the master or, at least, for failing to respond properly to what he knew about the master. He was supposed to have understood that the master was a man interested in a return on his investment, one always seeking to increase his holdings and, therefore, not content to have any of his resources lying idle or being used in a nonproductive manner.

Second, the unprofitable servant was held accountable for the misuse of certain resources with which he had been entrusted. If he had truly understood his master's nature, he would have acted more responsibly in the disposition of his master's assets. He would not have deployed them in so cautious and unproductive a manner.

The unprofitable economist in this story was simply more concerned for his own safety and well-being than for the desires of his master. He had little or no concern for his master's character and no faith in either the master's manner of doing business or his goals and objectives. He squandered the opportunity provided by the resources he had been given because he wished above all else to preserve his personal well-being (v. 25). As a result he was given to understand that he could expect no long-range benefits to accrue to him from the master's business, and he was rejected as a manager in the economy of that great man.

The two profitable servants, on the other hand, are seen to have properly inventoried the economic opportunity before them, rightly understood the master's expectations and manner of doing business, and reaped the harvest of increased economic resources and personal satisfaction. It is certain that these two would be entrusted with greater opportunities in the future, with even greater expected returns in profits and self-fulfillment.

It is of such stuff as this that we must be if we are to change the world by means of the economics of God.

Principles of God's Economics

There are seven principles that taken together can help us to become responsible managers of the time, talents, resources, and opportunities with which we have been entrusted by God. To the extent that we labor to understand these truths and to apply them in our everyday lives, we can expect to be functioning in accordance with divine guidelines for bringing God's economy into being in our world.

1. *We must each one come to recognize and accept the economic responsibilities laid upon us by God.* We can no longer allow a casual or indifferent attitude toward economic matters to pervade our thinking. This is not to say that we must all train ourselves in the academic discipline of formal economics. Rather, it is to insist that we come to see our relationship with Jesus Christ as something much more than a merely spiritual enterprise. The salvation He has accomplished and the Lordship He brings to us are as large as the whole of our lives. This being so, we cannot allow ourselves to become so heavenly minded that we are of no earthly value to God's kingdom.

To take seriously our economic calling is to begin to see ourselves as managers of resources not our own. Paul asked of the Corinthians, "What hast thou that thou didst not receive?" (1 Cor. 4:7). Everything we have comes from God, and we must understand that God has not relinquished concern for the proper use of those things with which He has entrusted us. Since everything either conduces to or detracts from the glory of God, this includes everything over which we have been made managers in God's name. God is concerned to know how we will manage the resources and affairs of our lives. Let us not be found guilty of a flippant or indifferent attitude toward these economic responsibilities. If we are to have others consider us as "God's economists," we must first recognize and accept that responsibility ourselves (1 Cor. 4:1-2).

2. *We must focus our concern as God's economists on the objectives He has determined to be of most importance.* The great temptation, of course, is to become so carried away with our own shortsighted perceptions of what is economically significant that we fail to consider the overarching concerns of the Master as we reach for our wallet, mark a date on our calendar, consider a business transaction, or enter into any of the myriad of economic opportunities that regularly come our way.

The two guideposts for economic activity that God has established are both simple and profound, micro- and macro-economic in their focus. First, God has said that our economic activity must contribute to the establishment of His order, harmony, beauty, and grace as pertains especially to the impersonal aspects of the creation. This was set forth from the beginning when God told Adam to fill the earth, subdue it, and exercise dominion over it in its totality (Gen. 1:28). This mandate has never been revoked. In the days of Adam and Eve this guiding principle comprehended their work—both physical and intellectual (Gen. 2:15-20)—their interpersonal relationships, their outlook on the creation round about them (Gen. 2:9), and their anticipated use of its resources (Gen. 2:10-12). It suggested to them how they should apportion the time that had been given to them. Any time not directly spent in subduing the earth and bringing God's order, harmony, beauty, and grace to bear upon it was time wasted. Any energy expended, except for that goal, was energy dissipated. At the end of each day we might imagine that God came to Adam and asked, "Adam, My son, what have you done this day that has contributed to the bringing about of My order, My harmony, My beauty, and My grace amid the splendors of this creation with which I have entrusted you?"

This is a question that we, too, must take seriously. As we think back each night on the work we have done, the reading and conversation into which we have entered, the money we have spent, and the innumerable tasks we have undertaken, to what extent are we confident that these have conduced to the glory of God, who entrusted them to our management for that day?

The second guidepost bears more directly on the personal aspects of the creation, namely, the men and women with whom we have contact each and every day of our lives. Our responsibility to them is summarized in the Great Commission of Jesus Christ. We are to do everything in our power to help them become disciples of the Lord (Matt. 28:18-20). Everything that we say must be so construed as to attract them to God (Col. 4:6; Eph. 4:29). All that we do must cause them to wonder about the goodness and greatness of our God (Matt. 5:16). And we must be prepared as God leads us to tell them the Good News of Jesus Christ and His love for sinful men (2 Tim. 4:2). As faithful managers of the relationships and interpersonal opportunities with which we are entrusted each day, we must be careful that they are pursued for the sake of the gospel above all.

As we keep these two guideposts in mind, we will be better

able on a day-in, day-out basis to manage the whole of our lives according to the overarching objectives of God in His economic plan for His people and His creation.

3. *We must maintain an updated inventory of our economic resources and opportunities.* The apostle Paul puts it this way: "See then that ye walk circumspectly, not as fools, but as wise, Redeeming the time, because the days are evil" (Eph. 5:15–16). One of the regular duties of ranchers and cattlemen is to walk the fences of their spreads. This requires them, on a regular basis, to survey the entire perimeter of their property and gives them a look at their herds and holdings from the outside in. They are able to spot problems, areas where shoring-up is needed, and places where new grazing lands might soon be developing. Walking the fences of their property provides an excellent analogy for us concerning the meaning of Paul's instruction.

Paul intends for us regularly to "walk the fences" of our day-to-day experience. We are to "walk circumspectly," that is, with a view to the entire horizon of our experience. We are to take note of opportunities, responsibilities, relationships, and resources, which in these evil days are to be entered into or deployed as wise men and "not as fools." This means that we will "redeem our time" with respect to these matters, making certain that we are using or pursuing them in a way that extracts them from their context of potential evil and redeems them for purposes of godliness and righteousness, a goal in accord with the overall objectives of God's economic plan.

Undoubtedly the best place for us to "walk the fences" of our lives is in prayer. In prayer we do not walk alone. Rather, God walks with us, and together we examine the people, resources, commitments, opportunities, and responsibilities with which He will be entrusting us that day. We want to learn to see these things from His perspective, with a view to His goals and objectives, and with a renewed resolve to manage the affairs of our lives in a comprehensive and responsible manner. As we walk the fences of our daily experience with God, inventorying the totality of our responsibilities as His managers, we will begin to discover new ways of redeeming the whole of our lives for His purposes and glory.

4. *As we enter the actual arena of economic activity, we must seek the desires of Christ in our every undertaking.* We might also

say that we are to seek "first the kingdom of God, and his righteousness" (Matt. 6:33) in every area of our lives.

But how will we be able to know whether or not we are really desirous of seeing our every activity pursued according to the kingdom purposes of Christ?

There are four questions we can ask about any opportunity or undertaking with which we are faced on any given day. The answers to each individual question will be more or less clear, according to the type of activity and the sincerity with which we ask them. Taken together, these questions can provide practical guidance for us in any sphere of our experience. They can help us genuinely to seek the realization of Christ's kingdom through the economic activities of our everyday lives.

The first question is "Can I honestly say that I am entering into this activity in full knowledge that Christ is on the throne in the midst of it?" Whether the activity in question is the purchase of a new car, a business deal or transaction, an interview or a meeting, we are to do all things "heartily, as to the Lord" (Col. 3:23). We cannot expect Christ to bless anything that we seek to accomplish "on the sly," that is, without having truly looked at it with reference to how Christ the King might feel about it. So much of what redounds to our regret, disadvantage, or misery could be avoided if we would simply take the time to search out an honest answer to this first question.

The second question is "Am I certain that this activity shows forth the truth of Christ?" In order to be able to answer this question, we must turn to the Word of God. We must take more seriously those passages that seem to have a bearing on such matters as business practices, purchases, and contracts. We are going to have to explore more deeply the subtle teachings of God's Word in the area of interpersonal relationships. If we are to be the "light of the world," it will require that the Light of God's Word show through in everything we do. Yet, it will be only as we ask this second question as a regular part of our economic behavior that this will begin to come to pass.

The third question is "Is this undertaking truly designed to minister grace to all parties concerned?" It is altogether unbecoming of Christian men and women to seek to arrange matters of business, finances, or personal relationships strictly for their own benefit. We must seek for others at least the same amount of blessing we seek for ourselves. We cannot expect that the blessings of God's kingdom will obtain where the selfishness and deceit of our sinful natures yet hold sway. The Golden Rule each of us learned in Sunday school as children is as valid for the whole of our lives as for any individual part.

The final question to ask in seeking the desires of Christ in our every undertaking is "Can I clearly see how this activity will conduce to the expansion of the kingdom of Christ?" Undoubtedly, this will be the hardest question of all to answer. Who can predict, regardless of our sincerity or care in planning, what will or will not occur in the future? At best, we can hope that the rationale behind our economic decisions will reveal intent on our part to further the work of Christ. Only we ourselves can truly know whether or not our motives in any situation or relationship are Christ-centered instead of self-serving in nature. But, if we will persist in asking ourselves this question with respect to all our responsibilities, opportunities, and activities, we might expect that we will tend more and more to seek the desires of Christ in all things.

5. *We must look for a return on our investment that is consistent with the Master's desires.* We must ask ourselves, "What does God want to see produced by my time, talents, and energies?" The answer seems to lie in three primary areas.

First, God appears to be interested in increased "profitability." That is, He is zealous for more and more of the activities and opportunities of human experience to come under the management umbrella of those who honor His purposes. Paul talks about our taking captive "every thought to the obedience of Christ" (2 Cor. 10:5). We take this to mean that God is interested in seeing the mind-set of Jesus Christ beginning to pervade more and more of the ideas, thoughts, and plans of men. Paul also says that in the saving work of Christ on the cross, God was reconciling all things unto Himself (Col. 1:20). He is reclaiming the whole of the lost world for His dominion, even as He originally charged Adam and Eve. We are profitable servants of God to the extent that our activities, relationships, and responsibilities are undertaken so as to contribute to that recapturing and reclaiming. The talents we have been given in order to serve God are meant to produce more of the same. We must focus our energies on a return on investment consistent with the profit-seeking desires of God.

Second, God has determined that His kingdom will expand

irrepressibly among men and nations, like leaven worked throughout three loaves of bread (Matt. 13:33). Where God's kingdom goes, His power and authority reign. Therefore, we seek the returns that God has in mind when we consciously strive to make our every undertaking contribute to the expansion of God's rule among men. Is it a business proposition we are considering? Let us determine that to the fullest of our ability, the glory of God will be kept at its center and His ways of doing business followed to the fullest. Is it a purchase we are thinking about? Let us ask how that purchase will make us more profitable to the kingdom of God and to its expansion among the people with whom we work and associate. Whatever it may be, let us determine that the rule of God will be in the midst of it, for this is His desire for our lives.

Third, we achieve returns consistent with the desires of the Master when they conduce to our own personal fulfillment as people who seek to be God's economists in the whole of our lives. It is the clear teaching of the Scriptures that there is no greater joy, no greater peace, no greater sense of purpose and meaning, than that which is found in becoming all that we have been created to be in Jesus Christ. As we seek to realize God's purposes in the whole of our lives, we will find His joy and His peace taking ever-deeper root in our hearts. This is as it should be for us who have been made complete in Jesus Christ and who are the recipients of His peace (Col. 2:10; John 14:27).

We can know that we are truly seeking God's returns on the investment of our time, talents, and energies when we have in mind these ideas of profitability, kingdom expansion, and personal fulfillment in the will of God.

6. *We must be ever mindful of our individual responsibility for the "all things" with which we have been entrusted.* If, as Paul says, "all things" are ours, and we are Christ's (1 Cor. 3:22–23), we have an obligation to make certain that the things of Christ be put to His proper service. A day of reckoning is coming for each and every one of us. We will be required to render an accounting of what we have done with the things we were given. On the foundation of Christ in our lives, some of us will build works of wood, hay, and stubble; those who are wiser will construct works of gold, silver, and precious stones (1 Cor. 3:11–12). Yet, none of us will be able to say, "I did not know,"

or "I had no opportunity to do better," or "I had to look out for myself," or any other of the hundred and one excuses that men give for not attending to the management of their lives according to the priorities and principles of Christ. We must each shoulder our individual responsibility to develop to the fullest our economic accountability before God for the things He has given us. Only thus will we be able to avoid the purging fires in that day of reckoning.

7. *Finally, we must maintain a realistic attitude about our economic responsibilities and achievements in this life.* We must come to see that we are all, regardless of the degree of our success or busy-ness, "unprofitable servants" (Luke 17:10). When we have done all that we can, it will be nothing more than what was expected of us. It will be the bare minimum of our debt to God, who paid such a high price to give us the privilege of knowing and serving Him. Thus, throughout our every effort to live as God's economists, we must see our utter dependence on His mercy and grace. Do we gain much in the way of souls for the kingdom? It is only God in His Spirit at work through us, bringing His own unto Himself. Do we acquire great riches and share them selflessly with the people of God everywhere? It is only His mercy and love at work within us, showing the zeal and compassion of the Savior in the works of our hands. Do we gain the esteem of men, become known for our kindness and love, acquire business empires, invest with the Midas touch, or manage others to the fullest use of their resources and capabilities? Let us quickly confess that the only profit that comes through such noble achievements is that which God grants for His own glory. We are all unprofitable servants, for there would be no hope of a godly economy beginning to be manifest among us were it not for the tireless and powerful working of God within those of us who have come to know Him (Phil. 2:12–13). This is the reality of our lives in Him. We must never lose sight of this fact.

God's Economists

There is a way of managing the affairs of men, a system of economics, that is certain to result in the maximum good for mankind and the most propitious use of the natural and human resources of this planet. We may call it the economics of God. It is a way of living and of conducting our affairs that takes seriously the claim of God to be the Lord of all of life, the Master of every aspect of human life and interest. It is a way of living which can show forth His beauty, goodness, justice, and truth at the same time it provides a wealth of blessedness to those who seek its implementation. We are God's economists, those who have been called to the proper management of His resources, His time, His talents, and the opportunities He gives us so as to achieve His purposes among men. If we can engender the necessary commitment on the part of God's people to the way of living that He intends, we can change the world.

Questions for Study or Discussion

1. Draw up a "spread-sheet" of your economic life by listing as many as possible of the "all things" of your life under the following headings:

Relationships   Responsibilities   Roles   Possessions   Opportunities

2. Now go back over that list and put a check mark by any of those items that you feel are not yet being managed according to the economic plans of God.

3. Consider each of those areas you checked and briefly describe a plan for bringing it under the management of God's economic principles.

For Further Reading

Blamires, Harry. *The Christian Mind.* Ann Arbor, Mich.: Servant Books, 1978.

Smith, Fred. *You and Your Network.* Waco, Tex.: Word Books, 1984.

7

God, Government, and Liberty

Government Encroachment

In our day it seems that almost everywhere we turn we run into government. More and more local, state, and federal governments are intruding themselves into our everyday lives. Families and individual wage earners bemoan the almost regular imposition of new and diverse forms of taxation. Corporations and businessmen grapple with regulatory agencies and hiring quotas. Manufacturers cringe at the introduction of every new government-mandated standard or guideline. Private schools and a whole host of tax-exempt organizations continually jockey to stay on the "good side" of the Internal Revenue Service. Courts break up school districts and foul up the legal system through petty technicalities and starry-eyed optimism concerning the rehabilitation of hard-core criminals. New laws, new regulations, new statutes, new guidelines, and new standards are constantly put forward "for the public good," as if the public could not survive without a healthy dose of revised legislation at regular intervals.

We are literally being hedged in, dressed down, and shoved around by government on every side. At least, that's the way it can seem at times.

Certainly every one of us has had occasion to pause and reflect on the ubiquity of government in our daily lives. Sometimes it seems as though we can hardly do anything or go anywhere without some kind of license, permit, sticker, or pass. We are becoming increasingly conscious of the watchful eye—and the heavy hand—of the government upon us.

Is this as it ought to be? Is this the ideal of "life, liberty, and the pursuit of happiness" that the founding fathers intended our government to provide? Or have we come to the place in our national history where it is perhaps time for some serious re-thinking on the part of all Americans concerning the meaning of responsible government?

The architects of American democracy labored to construct a political system that would allow for maximum individual freedom and minimal government control. The United States Constitution represents a most outstanding example of that ideal. It is a document that is extremely realistic and practical in its understanding of human nature. It acknowledges our tendency to sin and protects us from one another and from the tyranny of government. Furthermore, the Constitution is most optimistic in its regard for human potential. It seeks to give the maximum amount of room to individuals and institutions to develop their productive capabilities in relative freedom from governmental interference. And it acknowledges the need of a people for a national identity formed in the forge of personal freedoms, spiritual values, and interstate cooperation. Of all the documents of government that have ever appeared in the course of human history, the United States Constitution is the most brilliant and most eminently workable.

Yet, in our day, that majestic instrument has been pushed aside. Under the rubric of such phrases as "welfare," "relief," "public good," "environmental concern," and "social justice," the stability and freedoms of the Constitution have been gradually replaced by a many-tentacled, thousand-eyed government that sets itself forth as the panacea for every human ill.

As responsible citizens, called to be the world changers of this generation, we must examine this condition anew. We must come to a better understanding of the meaning of responsible government. We must consider whether truly responsible government is a retrievable commodity. And we must ask what will be required of responsible citizens in order to restore the vision that so inspired this nation's founding fathers.

The Bible sets forth some very clear criteria for responsible government. Woven throughout the pages of the Book are the principles and ideals that formed the thinking of those who framed our American system of government. We cannot return our nation to its proper constitutional basis without understanding those biblical guidelines. Let us consider those teachings.

Biblical Principles of Government

Certainly, the clearest teaching of the Bible concerning government is that it is the creation of God. No legitimate and responsible government takes power or authority unto itself. For "the powers that be are ordained of God" (Rom. 13:1). He is the source of their power; they are responsible to Him. Thus, no government can be said to be acting responsibly if it fails to acknowledge its own accountability to God.

The founders of this nation recognized that "a firm reliance on divine Providence" would be necessary to create a responsible government for the new nation. They had statements about that dependence engraved on their currency, etched into the cornerstones of their public buildings, written into their state constitutions, and institutionalized in chaplaincies for their houses of government. They knew that no government could serve its people in a responsible manner if it had an indifferent, cavalier attitude concerning its accountability to God.

How far we have come from those noble beginnings! Today our government casts a wary eye on those individuals and churches that take seriously their prophetic responsibility to hold governments accountable to God. It makes a mockery of public celebrations of religious holidays, crumbling under the pressure of special-interest groups and powerful individuals. And, in the name of education, government sponsors a religion of secular humanism, which exalts man as his own god and shuts all other faiths out of the pedagogical arena.

Clearly this is a government that has all but forgotten its responsibilities to God. It has abandoned the vision of the fathers. Can it be any wonder that such a government would experience so few constraints on its tendencies to intrude into the everyday lives and affairs of its citizens?

The Scriptures also teach that a responsible government exists to further the cause of good, that is, that which conforms to the desires of God (Rom. 13:4). Paul seemed to think that any government so committed would promote a social context in which the church could exist in quiet, peaceableness, godliness, and honesty (1 Tim 2:1–2). Government should not inhibit the work of the church in bringing the peace and reign of Christ to bear upon the lives of men and women. On the contrary, as part of its responsibility to God, civil authority must provide an environment in which those ends can be pursued to the maximum degree.

Yet, in our day, disturbing accounts surface from time to time that seem to indicate our government is failing in this responsibility. Churches have been padlocked, Christian schools closed, street preachers jailed, home Bible studies prohibited, and Christian literature proscribed. Is this responsible government— government that exists to minister the desires of God to its people?

A further responsibility of government is the suppression of evil. Government is called to be "a terror" to evil works (Rom. 13:3). If good is to flourish and justice prevail, evil must be opposed, suppressed, and destroyed. It is the responsibility of government to fulfill this obligation, since it bears the sword as a ministry of God, "a revenger to execute wrath upon him that doeth evil" (Rom. 13:4).

But is this what we see in the government of our land today? Do we not see a government which merely scolds evil-doers, when the clear need is that they be suppressed? Do we not see a government dangerously courting the favor of evil in international garb in the communist nations of this earth?

Is this responsible government—government acting on behalf of God to resist evil for the sake of good? Certainly not. We have fallen far away from those noble ideals of justice and right so eloquently and clearly set forth in the Constitution.

Finally, responsible government may neither aggrandize itself at public expense nor arrogate unto itself prerogatives belonging to God alone (Deut. 17:14–17; 1 Chron. 21:21–25; Acts 12:20–23). It is the responsibility of government to recognize and accept the limits and extent of its power. It must not unjustly enlarge itself against its citizens. And it must not aspire to divert unto itself the honor or duty that is God's alone.

In our day government is failing in both these charges. It

freely imposes taxes or dilutes the value of its currency in order to prop up politically motivated budgets. It robs its citizens in unfair and unequal tax schemes. It reserves to itself the privilege of defining right and wrong, truth and falsehood, life and death. It claims to own all the land by "eminent domain," thus clearly scorning the Word of God (Ps. 24:1). And it claims the right to determine what is and is not proper for the children of the land, ultimately drawing them unto itself rather than letting them come to Jesus Christ.

Truly our nation's government has strayed from biblical paths. It has broken loose from its constitutional moorings and is adrift on a sea of uncertainty and danger. It has abandoned its responsibility to God, for the sake of political expediency and mere self-perpetuation.

Yet, our government is not past retrieval. Responsible citizens, working according to biblical guidelines, can yet restore civil authority to its proper orientation.

Restoring Our Government

It will take true world changers to rise to this task. How will such responsible citizens be known among us? What actions will they take to restore government to its rightful, responsible place?

First of all, and most basically, responsible citizens must pray for their government. Following Paul's exhortation in 1 Timothy 2:1-3, they must recognize that all their efforts to restore government to a place of true accountability before God must be grounded in "supplications, prayers, intercessions, and giving of thanks" for those who are in authority over them. Specifically, we are to pray that God will give our government the prudence and wisdom it requires, so that His people "may lead a quiet and peaceable life in all godliness and honesty." This simple prayer request can become a standard by which we measure the government's effectiveness in ministering the will of God among us. To what extent and in what specific ways do governmental actions and decisions either contribute to or militate against the realization of these goals?

Second, the conscientious citizen cannot be content merely to pray for the powers-that-be. Responsible citizens must labor to influence government on behalf of the cause of the gospel. Nowhere is this duty more visible in the New Testament than in Paul's various defenses before the governors of Palestine (especially Acts 24:10-26 and 26:26-29). In this example we notice especially that Paul "reasoned by righteousness, temperance, and judgment to come" (Acts 24:25), seeking to persuade Felix of the truths that are important for governments to promote. If our own errant government is to be returned to a place of responsible functioning in the eyes of God, it must endorse and adopt policies and programs consistent with the righteousness, temperance, and judgment of God. Such will only be the case as responsible citizens take it upon themselves—in letters, demonstrations, public gatherings, and in polling places—to stand squarely for such matters and insist that government do the same.

Third, to the extent that government's policies and programs are consistent with the good purposes of God as revealed in His Word, they must be outspokenly supported and wholeheartedly obeyed (Rom. 13:1-4). Christian world changers are not anarchists. They do not criticize government for the mere sake of criticism alone. Their efforts in that vein are purposive, and, to the extent that governmental activities are consistent with those purposes, responsible citizens must exhibit and promote obedience to their civil leaders.

Yet, the responsible citizen's obedience to government must not be without qualification or reservation. We must always bear in mind that our loyalty to any government is always strictly secondary in nature. We owe a higher allegiance to God and render no faithful service to Him if we slavishly and silently adhere to government policies that contravene His will (John 18:35-36).

Especially in this day, when the activities of government have drifted so far from the original intentions of our nation's founders, must we be clear about our responsibilities to oppose the government when necessary. Specifically, we must know what actions are prescribed for us as legitimate means of protest against the ungodly policies of government.

First, it is our responsibility to protest in a prophetic manner such activities and decisions that either clearly transgress the bounds of morality or inhibit our ability to serve God (2 Sam. 12:1-10; Acts 4:18-20). Such a protest may be carried out by means of the spoken and written word, or in public rallies, assemblies, and demonstrations. In each case, however, we must make certain that a clear and specific activity is targeted. It is characteristic of anarchists and radicals of all sorts that their protests are vague, nonspecific, and based more on emotion than on sound judgment. Such must not be the case among responsible citizens organized to protest some policy or action of government. All involved must clearly understand the rationale behind and purpose for the activity of protest. Otherwise we shall be unable to know in which specific direction acceptable change might move.

Second is defiance (Acts 4:19-20; Dan. 3:1-18). After protest has been registered and received, we must make it clear to the powers-that-be that we shall not submit to their authority in the area in question. We must make certain that they understand that we intend to obey God and will not join them in disobedience to His will. When government has adopted policies and practices contrary to the will of God, it has defaulted on its responsibilities and violated its trust. We are irresponsible if we fail to point out such areas and to serve notice of our determination not to submit to them.

Finally, our actions in protest of government policy may lead us into some act of civil disobedience (Acts 4:18-33; Dan. 6:4-10). Yet we must never adopt such a policy for sheer rebellion's sake. This is anarchism, not responsible citizenship. When disobedience to governmental action is justified, it must occur as the natural outworking of our acts of obedience to God. If and when we make a conscious decision to defy civil authority, we must make certain that our disobedience to government is at the same time an act of obedience to some clearly specified teaching of God's Word.

Much prayer and forethought must go into any action we might adopt in seeking to oppose the government. We must make certain before God that our choices of action are responsible and clearly directed at restoring government to its proper place of accountability in His sight.

The Road to Enduring Freedom

Let us observe that responsible citizens, especially Christian world changers, must not hesitate to exercise their rights, obligations, duties, and talents in the service of responsible government. We must become involved in the political activities of the various national parties. We must not shy away from open and active involvement in campaigning for those candidates we believe will labor diligently to restore our government to its constitutional base. We must vote responsibly and consistently and stay in touch with our lawmakers so as to continually urge and exhort them in a godly direction. We must become more astute in our understanding of godly government and more aware of the complex issues before us. The most effective means to morally accountable government is to motivate responsible citizens to perform all their obligations, urging and leading them to render unto the government that which it ought legitimately expect from all its citizens (Matt. 22:21; cf. Dan. 6:1–3).

The road to enduring freedom lies in the direction of responsible government. If we are to be done with the peering, prodding, prying, and presumption of governments grown too big for their own good as well as ours, we must know what the Word of God specifies as legitimate for governments before Him. And we must commit ourselves to functioning as conscientious citizens, working to restore a proper balance between legitimate rule and personal freedom.

Responsible citizens make for responsible governments. Let the world changers of this generation commit themselves to both.

Questions for Study or Discussion

1. On what basis did believers oppose the actions of their governments in each of the following situations? What form did their opposition take?

Daniel 6:4–16

Acts 4:5–20

2. How do you suppose the early believers evaluated whether or not their governments were providing for "a quiet and peaceable life in all godliness and honesty" (1 Tim. 2:2) for their people?

3. Make a list of all the *specific* ways that you as a Christian can be involved in helping government to be more responsible.

For Further Reading

Singer, C. Gregg. *A Theological Interpretation of American History.* Phillipsburg, N.J.: Presbyterian and Reformed Publishing Co., 1981.

Whitehead, John W. *The Second American Revolution.* Elgin, Ill.: David C. Cook Publishing Co., 1982.

8

Advocates of Truth

"And Gladly Teach"

Geoffrey Chaucer's *Canterbury Tales* represent a majestic achievement in the use of the English language to capture and preserve for the ages a picture of a world long since perished. In these unfinished vignettes Chaucer presents the beauty and diversity—as well as the baseness and the glory—of life in medieval England.

The tales are set in the context of a group of pilgrims making their way to Canterbury for religious purposes. The various members of the group concoct the tales to pass the time on their journey. In these stories, together with the description of the characters provided in the prologue, the reader is treated to a colorful potpourri of English life in the late fourteenth century. Here we are provided with a look into the vocations, culture, diversions, values, ideals, people, and institutions that characterized an entire nation.

Among the most vivid and esteemed of the characters in the Canterbury entourage is the clerk, a young Oxford scholar. For Chaucer, this student was the embodiment of all that was noble and good in fourteenth-century education. He is the very epitome of English university learning. Clearly Chaucer, himself an Oxford man, had a high regard for the educational institutions of his day.

What kind of picture does Chaucer give us of English education?

The clerk is portrayed as being of a humble and meager visage, a thoroughly unworldly young man who had turned his back on all mundane pleasures for the calling of scholarship. We are told that he preferred the company of books—and, especially, of Aristotle, for medieval students the greatest of all scholars—to the riches and pleasures of his day. He had little money, and what he was able to secure from his friends—perhaps by tutoring—was immediately reinvested in the furthering of his knowledge and education. He was a man of few words, but when he spoke it was concisely and considerately, with reverence and perfect grammar, and always in a manner that tended to inculcate moral virtue.

Only one passion consumed this clerk as much as learning, and that was the passion to teach others, to introduce them to the mysteries and glories of knowledge. Truly, here was a serious advocate of medieval learning. Appropriately, Chaucer's description of this clerk ends, "And gladly would he learn, and gladly teach."

Here, then, is personified for the ages a tradition of teaching and learning that Chaucer saw as noble and exalted. It was an education that understood the transiency of material possessions and prized the perfections of truth. This system of learning thrived on hard work and conduced to the moral edification of its beneficiaries. It was a pedagogy of precision, sacrifice, and reserve.

Teaching and Learning Today

I wonder: How might some modern-day Chaucer portray the system of education currently dominating the American cultural scene? What form might some contemporary educational personification take?

One has only to peruse the literature and classrooms of American education today to imagine a portrait that would be something less than flattering. Despite the many outstanding examples of dedication and competency presiding behind the lecterns of American classrooms, the vast bulk of the evidence indicates that our educational process is in the throes of a crisis.

What began under the close supervision of parents, pastors, and local community leaders for the edification and ennobling

of the generations to come has degenerated into a monstrous
state-run system of mediocrity and moral relativism in which the
brightest and the best are stifled and smothered by requirements
geared to the abilities of the lowest common denominator of
students. Massive teachers' unions, ostensibly organized to further the cause of quality instruction, have turned the classroom
into a political circus in which traditional values and institutions
are subverted or openly mocked. Textbooks founded upon eternal truths have been discarded for those designed to promote
relativity in values and views of American history. These totally
ignore the Christian roots of this nation's beginnings. School
buildings, teachers, and fellow students are physically assaulted
and abused by learners who are fed up with being caged in a
system perceived as having no relevance for their lives. Teachers
who are motivated by personal gain or political bias; school
property subjected to incessant vandalism; philosophical intran-
sigence in the classroom; administrative buffoonery; gross
immorality presented as having educational significance; high-
school graduates who are unable to read; and the ever-present
and meddlesome involvement of government in the learning
process all suggest a personification that would be vastly different from the noble and serene lad whom Chaucer described.

American education has been characterized by the National
Commission on Excellence in Education as contributing to making this a nation at high risk of frittering away its greatness and
its future for the sake of pedagogical gimmickery, "pass/fail-
ism," moral absurdity, spiritual sterility, and assorted other educational tomfooleries of demonstrably negative impact. Such a
system will most definitely help shape the world in which we
live, but we will surely rue the changes this education brings.

Is there a future in the American educational process for
those who truly desire to learn? Will those who gladly seek
learning today be able to find a setting of sufficient seriousness
and purpose to satisfy their longings? Unless the true world
changers of this generation step into the chaos of modern education and begin to bring a new order and meaning, I am afraid
there is not much hope for positive answers to these questions.

We who are committed to bringing a new way of life to the
people of our generation must begin to take more seriously our
roles in the work of education. Through education we preserve,

deepen, and perpetuate our spiritual and cultural heritage. And, as never before in American history, that heritage really needs to receive a wide hearing. To that end, a comprehensive and effective educational effort must be undertaken, an endeavor in which we all have a part.

A Qualitative Difference

But, one may object, is there not a great deal of activity already being pursued in the name of Christian education? What are we missing that we need to add? The Sunday school has just celebrated its two-hundredth anniversary and appears to be alive and growing. A Christian day-school movement is under way, attracting thousands of new students each week. Bible and Christian liberal arts colleges are more popular than ever. When you add all the various types of seminars, Bible studies, correspondence courses, youth groups, and midweek Bible schools, together with a burgeoning traffic in audio cassettes and video cassettes—not to mention Christian radio and television!—what more could we discover to do?

A fair question. Yet, mere activity alone can never suffice to satisfy the criteria by which we measure our effectiveness. Any work in Christian education must always be *unto* something, a means to an end and not an end in itself. From this perspective, the mere fact that our frenzy of Christian educational activity seems to be making so slight an impact in our contemporary culture and society suggests, even for all our efforts, that something more needs to be done.

It may well be that what is needed is not so much something *quantitatively* more as something *qualitatively* more. Although progress in morality and true learning necessarily will require more of everything mentioned above, a mere multiplication of our efforts will make but little difference toward changing the world, unless we begin to take some radically new approaches to the *way* in which we educate.

It is precisely in this manner that each of us as world changers can begin to contribute more effectively to the improvement of our educational endeavors. As members of the believing community and participants in its educational activities, we must each one assume a more purposeful and active role in bringing about the kind of education that truly changes lives in positive ways.

But to do that we need some guaranteed guidelines such as can only come from the Word of God. In obedience to His commands and in dependence upon His promises, we can begin to approach our work in Christian education in a manner more consistent with His will.

Some Biblical Guidelines

Let's look at some examples of the kind of guidelines which can help us bring about a more world-changing Christian education.

In Genesis 18:19 a very clear and most important component of effective Christian education is set forth. Speaking of Abraham, God says, "For I know him, that he will command his children and his household after him, *and they shall keep the way of the Lord, to do justice and judgment . . ."* (italics added). Here God endorses the passing on to subsequent generations of His commandments, to the end that those generations learn to live in ways reflective of His character. That is, God wants our educational efforts to be directed toward behavioral ends consistent with His will.

It is not enough in our work in education, at whatever level or in whatever context, to concentrate on either the mere transmission of factual data or the creation in our learners of some sense of personal well-being or peace. The purpose of our instruction must be to affect the behavior—the life-style—of learners in such a way that they demonstrate more consistently and thoroughly the marks of godly character.

So much of our work in Christian education appears to be satisfied with meeting only two of the three requirements of true learning. We seem content either just to pass along a certain amount of information or to provide some sort of "mountaintop experience" for our learners. To be sure, both knowledge and some sort of affective experience are critical aspects of true learning. Both the mind and heart must be appropriately engaged before the will can be exercised in the direction of a changed life.

It is the changed life, however, that is the ultimate goal of our learning. We must insist of those involved in the work of Christian education that they concentrate on a quality of instruction that strives for changed lives. There will be no changed world without changed lives, and we will not be able to accomplish these ends until we begin more consciously to teach and to learn with this in mind.

Thus, it is not unreasonable for us to expect that our instructors—be they Sunday-school teachers, seminary professors, or Bible teachers—should have in mind specific areas of life and particular life-style applications for their students. We must be bold enough to ask them, "What are you hoping to teach me? What should I be expected to learn? How will this particular portion of God's Word affect my everyday life?" And we must be faithful and diligent to study and to learn so as to realize those changes. Our Christian education will be powerful unto a revitalized world only to the extent that we, following the clear teaching of God's Word, expect of ourselves and our teachers nothing less than specific learning objectives, goals described in terms of changes in our life-styles.

But even the noblest of life-style learning objectives can be to no lasting purpose unless we keep in mind a proper overall perspective for all our learning. Jesus said that our teaching and learning are to be coordinated unto the discipling of all the nations (Matt. 28:19-20). This single Great Commission must guide all our efforts. As a people whose liberties are being increasingly threatened and whose institutions have come under attack by the media and the courts, we cannot afford the luxury of spending our learning energies on mere frivolities or "self-stroking" enterprises. All our teaching and all our learning must be organized around one basic question: "How is this class, course, or study going to contribute toward making me a disciple and toward making disciples of others?"

So the question of specific goals and objectives must be kept before us at all times as we pursue our work in Christian education.

A second guideline that surfaces in the Scriptures has to do with the manner in which we select our teachers. Sometimes, perhaps because we are eager to provide some form of Christian education for everyone, in our efforts to secure teachers we give the impression that teaching is something anyone can do. Such, however, is not the testimony of the Bible.

The apostle James warns, "My brethren, be not many mas-

ters, knowing that we shall receive the greater condemnation"
(James 3:1). Here the apostle clearly suggests that teaching is
not a calling to which everyone may aspire. Effective teaching
requires a gift from God. It is not the province of all believers,
nor should it be treated as such. It is a mockery of true teaching
to recruit and "train" teachers just for the sake of augmenting
class rolls. Such approaches thrive on the claim that "anyone
can teach." Because such an approach debases teaching—making it a calling that because "anyone" can do it, nobody wants
to—potentially effective teachers can be discouraged from becoming involved in this enterprise, which has lost its distinctive-
ness. Paul taught that we should highly esteem those who labor
at teaching (1 Tim. 5:17). Yet, we only truly esteem that which is
in short supply. We need only compare our own attitudes, say,
toward sparrows and toward eagles to see the truth of this.

Thus, we must seek out those who truly possess the gift of
teaching and encourage and assist them in developing and using
it for a changed world.

Paul gives us three criteria we can use to identify and develop
effective teachers. In 2 Timothy 2:2 Paul tells us, "And the
things that thou hast heard of me among many witnesses, the
same commit thou to faithful men, who shall be able to teach
others also." Who will be able to teach others? First, those who
are good students, those quick to learn in a life-changing way
the great truths of God's Word. No one can be an effective
teacher who is not first of all an effective learner. As we search
for those who are potentially effective teachers, let us look first
to those who are quick and effective learners.

Second, effective teachers are also to be faithful. They must
study faithfully and should be expected to prepare diligently.
They must labor at getting to know their students well. And they
must be ever-involved in broadening the base of their knowledge
so as to be able continually to bring more light into their teaching. Effective teachers are faithful, and their faithfulness redounds to the benefit of their learners.

Thus, as we look about for those who can be expected to
become gifted teachers, let us seek out men and women who are
faithful with whatever God has given them to do in their lives. If
they are faithful in the small things of their everyday walk with
Christ, they will be faithful in the greater responsibilities of
teaching.

Finally, those who can be expected to become effective teachers will manifest some special abilities required by that calling. They will be able to learn the Word of God. They will evidence some talent to master a body of truth in an organized way. They will be able to communicate in an effective and winsome manner with others. In large part their ability to teach will derive from a combination of their faithfulness and the talents they demonstrate. To the extent that they are good leaders who are faithful in all things, their latent abilities can be channeled and developed to enable them to become effective teachers.

Rather than open the ranks of teaching to any who might wish to "have a go at it," let us follow the guidelines set forth in God's Word and insist that our teachers be of such a caliber and quality that they will be esteemed by all and effective in their labors unto a changed world. Our efforts at Christian education require the best that we can muster.

A third guideline evident in the Scriptures is that our teaching and learning must be closely tied to our everyday experience. This is most clearly seen in the ministry of our Lord Jesus Christ.

Jesus taught eternal, propositional truths in the most common of ways. He was no mere abstract theologian and gloried neither in philosophical terminology nor the language of professional dogmaticians. Jesus gave His audiences insight into the sovereign care of God by pointing to sparrows and lilies. He brought small children before His learners in order to talk about faith. Feasts and weddings, funerals and childbirths, quarrelings and betrothals, kingdoms and farms—all provided Jesus with opportunities to communicate eternal truths in familiar terms. Because He knew what was in every man and woman, Jesus could teach effectively by couching heavenly truth in earthly images. Those who would sponsor an educational endeavor that intends to change the world must work at communicating in the language and according to the level of understanding of their learners.

Jesus also focused His teaching on the most mundane of human experiences. He knew that God's truth was meant to affect everyday lives and to change ordinary patterns of behavior. Thus, He taught repentance to tax collectors and harlots, instructed the rich and their servants concerning their respective responsibilities, and gave advice to governors and fishermen alike. And always His practical instructions were framed in the context of the Great Commission.

In order to be able to teach in such a powerful and comprehensive manner, teachers must first of all commit themselves to thorough understanding of the truth that is to be communicated. We can only make God's truth intelligible to others if we are able to discover correlations and applications between those truths and our own experiences. Yet, only by thoroughly meditating upon and working through the subject we are to teach can we identify those places and consider how to communicate them to our learners.

But, second, this also requires a commitment to our learners, to discovering the things that are of interest or concern to them as well as the specific learning needs they have. Those who would teach must work at developing new relationships and new friendships with their learners. They must also work hard at being able effectively to communicate God's truth to them. Love demands that those who would teach must care so much for God's truth, as well as for their students, that they spare no effort to effect a proper matching of the two—and this can only be done around the everyday experiences of those who have come to learn.

Finally, the Scriptures are quite clear that no education will be productive of lasting change if it relies on anything other than the Holy Spirit for its ultimate success (1 John 2:27).

How great is the temptation in our day to think and act as though success in Christian education is a function of some human aspect of the teaching and learning process. We invest enormous sums of money in developing expensive and attractive curricula. As we clamor for the newest instructional tools and technologies, we celebrate the guaranteed virtues of this or that teaching method. We cry out, "If only we just had more films, flashier booklets, or better facilities—then we could really change the world!"

Yet, as significant as these things may be, they do not begin to compare with the importance of maintaining a prominent place for the Holy Spirit in our instruction. If our teachers do not learn how to depend upon Him, and if they fail to lead us to do the same, we shall not be able to bring about the quality of learning that our age requires. Only the Holy Spirit can lead us into all truth (John 16:13). Only the Holy Spirit comprehends the depths of the mind of God (1 Cor. 2:11). And only the Holy Spirit can teach us the things of Christ (John 14:26). Clearly, any program of education that intends to change the world after the pattern of God's Word must intimately and thoroughly involve the Holy Spirit in the teaching and learning process.

This we do, in the first place, through prayer. We must make certain that our work in Christian education is bathed in prayer. As we plan our programs, prepare for our classes, and participate together in the various learning enterprises that are the stuff of Christian education, let us make certain that prayer envelops all that we do. Through heartfelt and conscientious communion with the Spirit of God in prayer, we can tap into the power for true learning that will help make our educational undertakings truly effective.

But we must also depend upon the Holy Spirit, at work within us, for faith and obedience. We must look to Him to enable us to work out our own salvation, to be able to will and do God's good pleasure (Phil. 2:12–13). As we study and concentrate on specific changes, specific attitudes, and specific actions to be taken, it will only be as we look to the Spirit of God and step out in Him that we will find the power we need to change the world. We must act on the things we learn, believing that God, through His Spirit, will enable us to become all that He wants us to be. For this, we must call upon God's Spirit, looking to Him for strength and perseverance. Only thus will the power that can change the world begin to be unleashed in our lives.

Advocates of Truth

In a recent article in a leading educational journal, one of the most popular learning theorists of our day lamented the lack of an overall sense of purpose or meaning to American education. He indicated that it would be better if there were some full-blown world and life view in place somewhere that American education could measure itself against, even if that view involved belief in God and His overarching control of things. Yet, he went on, it is clear that even such positions as this have "no serious advocate" promoting their adoption today.

Is this the extent of the impact that our frenzied activity in

Christian education has been able to produce in this unbelieving world? "No serious advocate"? Clearly, either we have not been working hard enough, or we have not been working well enough. We prefer to believe it is the latter.

Yet, it is not too late to do something about it. If we can begin to take more seriously the setting and achieving of specific goals in education; if we are careful to develop only the best and most capable among us as our teachers; if we can concentrate on tying our learning closely to our lives; and if we can look consistently to the Holy Spirit to empower and guide us, we might just be able to revitalize our work in Christian education to such an extent that we can truly change the world.

"And gladly would he learn, and gladly teach." Let it be said of each one of us that we take seriously our involvement in the work of Christian education, regardless of what that may be. If we are to overcome the negative and destructive effects of contemporary humanistic education, we must begin today, right where we are, as teachers, students, parents, or sponsors of any form of Christian education. In the face of the present-day educational crisis we must each one strive to personify the kind of outlook on and commitment to the work of education that will show us to be truly serious advocates of a pedagogy that can be used of God to make all things new.

Questions for Study or Discussion

1. List below all the educational activities in which you are involved, either as a teacher or learner. Then, go back to each one and write one sentence explaining what your personal learning objective is for each case.

Activity   *Objective*

2. What does Paul say is involved in the process of learning in a manner consistent with our life in Christ? See Ephesians 4:20–24.

3. What does Paul say is one danger we need to be on guard against in the learning process in 2 Timothy 3:5–7?

For Further Reading

Gaebelein, Frank. *The Pattern of God's Truth.* Chicago: Moody Press, 1968.

Lewis, C. S. *The Abolition of Man.* New York: Macmillan, 1965.

Wolterstorff, Nicholas. *Educating for Responsible Action.* Grand Rapids, Mich.: Wm. B. Eerdmans Publishing Co., 1980.

9

How Does Your Garden Grow?

Woes in the Garden

Few aspects of American life have received more attention or been the object of more discussion in the media during recent months than the American worker. With unemployment recently running at the highest levels in years, new threats to job stability arising from overseas, concerns about quality being expressed on the part of labor and management alike, and the technological revolution looking as though it might put everyone's job up for grabs, it should not be surprising to discover that as a nation we are undergoing something of a "work identity crisis." The image of the American worker seems to be changing—from proud and unexcelled to indifferent and ineffective. Professionals who in former times would have been content for life in their chosen fields are setting out in new directions for new careers. White-collar crime is becoming a national scandal. Blue-collar crime is a way of life for many. Traditional jobs are disappearing, robots are taking the places of many on assembly lines, and hardly anyone ever seems content with his or her wages or working conditions. "Fewer hours!" "More benefits!" "Government subsidies!" These are the cries issuing forth from the workplaces of America in our day.

Clearly, all is not well with the American worker. Attitudes of self-centeredness and complacency have eroded the dignity of work in our nation. What used to be seen as a vocation, a calling to labor in a productive and useful occupation, has for many degenerated into nothing more than a mere job, a necessary evil that contributes only to the humdrum of human existence. Work, like so much else in American life, has lost all meaning beyond that of making a living. For many, their work has no greater short-range goal than the next payday, no more significant long-range objective than retirement. The biblical view of work as a uniquely human function, ordained of God and intended to redound to His glory, has all but been lost in our modern society.

Yet, it is precisely this ideal of work that the world changers of today must seek to recapture. It is up to the world changers of this generation to restore dignity and meaning to work. If our work is to be all that it can be in God's economy, we must begin to consider it anew from the vantage point of His Word. And to do that we will need to go back to the Garden, back to the beginning of man's calling to work, in order to discover again the beauty and significance of this uniquely human activity.

We say "uniquely human" for only humans have the capacity to work consciously toward the goal of glorifying God in their every task. Animals may perform certain kinds of work, but only a man or woman can know and conscientiously pursue work in order to set forth the beauty, wisdom, grace, and majesty of God. It is only from the perspective of work as a uniquely human function that we shall be able to gain a clearer understanding of the biblical teachings concerning work. It is only in the acknowledgment of and submission to those teachings that we will be able to rescue our work from the doldrums.

A Glimpse into the Garden

In Genesis, chapter two, we find the first teaching in the Scriptures concerning man's works. Some important points present themselves for our consideration.

First, notice that work is given to mankind by God (Gen. 2:15). Thus, work must be understood as having its origin in God's goodness. Work is not a curse. To see our own work as drudgery is to fail to understand its true nature and purpose. In giving us work, God invites us to share with Him in His own creative efforts, offering us the opportunity to perpetuate and expand the goodness and beauty He has initiated. In our work we continue the purposes of God, who pronounced His own work "very good" (Gen. 1:31) when He had at last finished it and handed it over to men and women to continue.

By our work we provide sustenance for ourselves and our loved ones and also manifest our own concern for the needs of others, those who "consume" the products of our labor. In work we express something of ourselves. In fact, in no other arena of human life is there such opportunity to set forth our individual sense of worth and concern for excellence and goodness than in our work. Furthermore, by our work we contribute to the overall economic health of our nation.

We must see our work as being done for the goodness of God, and we must approach it for the opportunities to show forth the goodness it affords.

Second, Scripture tells us that two kinds of work are appropriate for mankind. We are given both manual and intellectual labor (Gen. 2:15, 19). Keeping the Garden in shape was undoubtedly a challenging and tiring assignment. But what beauty could be displayed, what designs of symmetry set forth, what abundance of harvest reaped by the faithful physical labor of Adam's hands! Truly, there was glory to be revealed in manual labor.

On the other hand, naming the animals was an intellectual task. It required precise logic, descriptive language, systematic categorization, and a vast memory. What glories could be known in the process of describing the inhabitants of the animal kingdom!

How easily we can pit these two types of work against each other. How thoughtlessly we exalt one over the other. Both manual and intellectual labor have been given to us by God. Each has its place and each its unique function in bringing glory to Him. Let us study to see the virtues in each and to find ways of maximizing their complementarity.

Finally, we observe in this passage that there is simply too much work for one person to do all alone (Gen. 2:18–23). Although the institution of marriage is primarily in view here, the fact of Eve's being a "helpmeet" suggests the truth of our assertion. We need to learn the joys and the virtues of working harmoniously with others. We need to be able to recognize and accept our own shortcomings and limitations, to rely freely on others to help us complete our work and to make our strengths available to complement the wants and needs of others.

Guidelines for the Garden

We must ask ourselves: How do our gardens grow? How is it with us and our work? Do we regard our work as a good gift from God? Do we enter into it enthusiastically, striving for excellence? Do we accept our share of both manual and intellectual labor? Have we learned the art of working well with others? Is the glory of God—His beauty, wisdom, grace, and truth—clearly evident in the work that we do?

If we are honest, we will probably all admit to needing a little help in one or the other of these areas as far as our work is concerned. We want to suggest six guidelines that can help us realize more fully the biblical purpose for work. Understanding and beginning to implement these principles can revolutionize our approach to work and bring new meaning and purpose to the workplace.

1. *We must each one learn to see our work in its totality.* The work that we have been given to do is certainly broader than the job at which we work. We have been commissioned to bring the glory of God to fruition amid all circumstances of our lives and to show others how they may come to know God through faith in Jesus Christ (Gen. 1:26–28; Matt. 28:19–20). These two parameters define the scope of those labors and are the responsibility of everyone who names the name of Jesus Christ. For us to be content to have our God-appointed "work" satisfied only in our jobs is to fail to understand the scope of both the responsibilities and opportunities that have been given to us. Further, to limit our understanding of our work to our jobs alone is to disqualify those who are "retired" from contributing significantly to God's plan of work for His people. It is clear that we need to expand the horizons for our understanding concerning work.

But how can we develop a broader and more realistic view of our work? To properly understand and accomplish the work that has been assigned to us, we must see our work as organized around the various social institutions of which we are a part. Each of us travels in a variety of social spheres. For example, we may be members of a family, most of us will also have a regular job, and we are all citizens of this nation and members of the church of Jesus Christ. As many as five or six social institutions may be represented by our involvement in these units. Certainly, there are the home, the workplace, the marketplace, the nation, and the local church, and possibly the educational, charitable, and political domains. We are participating members in those spheres in which we choose to involve ourselves. Thus, we have a share in the responsibility for the work to be done there.

It is important to see that in each of these areas are social institutions toward which we have certain obligations and responsibilities. Our work of magnifying the glory of God and building others up in Jesus Christ comprehends all these commitments. Thus, the totality of our work is vastly larger than those commitments required by our jobs alone. We have work to do at home. There are labors of love to be fulfilled through the local church. If we are parents of schoolchildren and members of a PTA or school board, we have work to fulfill in these areas as well. We must labor to uphold and obey the laws of the land insofar as they are in accord with the Word of God, and we must work for the election of responsible political representatives.

Clearly, therefore, the totality of all our work must be kept in mind throughout the day. Through prayer and a circumspect life-style (Eph. 5:15–16), we will be able to identify our responsibilities more effectively and fulfill them in a comprehensive and godly manner. This is not to negate the importance of our jobs. Instead, it is to call for a more responsible overall approach to fulfilling our individual callings as laborers in the Garden of the Lord.

2. *We must learn to see the various aspects of our work according to their place in God's economy* (1 Cor. 10:31; Col. 3:17). Here we are calling for a proper prioritization of our work and a recognition of individual limitations. For each of us, our priorities and capabilities for work will be different. We must constantly question the eternal value of any individual aspect of our work and be ever mindful of the limits of what we as individuals can undertake at any given time.

Each of us has been uniquely gifted and called to fulfill certain responsibilities in God's Garden. Only through a proper assignment of priorities and an awareness of both our abilities and personal limits will we be able to labor to the maximum degree of effectiveness.

3. *We must learn to work toward specific goals, giving God the praise for each accomplishment.* This guideline derives immediately from the first two. The Bible encourages us to take an approach to our lives and our work that involves prayerful and careful forethought and planning. Moses instructs us "to number our days, that we may apply our hearts unto wisdom" (Ps. 90:12). Both Jesus and Paul evidenced careful planning in their ministries (cf. Matt. 21:1-3; Luke 22:7-12; Rom. 15:22-25). The apostle James warns, however, that all such planning must be undertaken in prayer, so as to keep our plans in their proper divine perspective (James 4:13-15).

There are numerous practical benefits to be gained from taking a planned approach to our work. Preparing a course of action helps to ensure that something will be accomplished as a result of our labors. The old maxim "Aim at nothing, and you'll hit it every time" contains a great deal of truth. Conversely, targeting specific goals can contribute to our realizing stated results. If we are careful to keep our objectives realistic, attainable, defined in terms of measurable outcomes, and in line with our priorities, we will be able to make real progress in all our labors for the Lord.

Planning helps to guarantee that we will waste as little time as possible. People are notorious time wasters. Either by simply "doing nothing" or by involving ourselves in activities that are merely frivolous or unproductive, we fritter away one of the greatest possessions bestowed upon God's people—time. For a graphic illustration of the truth of this, try this simple exercise: For one week keep a log of your waking moments. Every thirty minutes, write down what you did in the previous thirty minutes. At the end of the day, tally up the wasted time. Then, at the end of the week, add up the wasted time for each day. If you are like most people who have done this, you will be astounded at the hours of time that you regularly waste. Planning your work, and then working your plan, can help you avoid this.

Planning is a sure way to keep you prayerful and circumspect

concerning the responsibilities and opportunities that the Lord
brings to you. We will be more assured of keeping our priorities
current and the boundaries of our personal limitations in mind
if we will adopt a planning approach to the work we have been
given.

4. *Let us be careful to take advantage of the opportunities for
personal relationships and ministry that our work affords.* Gerard
Roche, perhaps the nation's leading recruiter of top executives,
has been quoted as saying, "Everyone I meet is a prospect, a
candidate, a reference, or a client." Roche takes a targeted approach to the people he meets, and so should we.

But how? How should we look at the people with whom we
come in contact in our work?

First, everyone we meet is a target for the love of Jesus Christ.
There is no excuse for today's world changers reaching out to
the people around them with anything other than the love of
God. This attitude of love will affect the way that we talk to
others (Col. 4:6) as well as the way that we relate to them (1 Pet.
2:17). The love of Christ can be the means to rich and rewarding
relationships with the people we encounter in the various
spheres of our work.

Further, everyone we meet will fall into one of two categories.
They will either be followers of Christ or people who are yet in
their sins. In either case, specific requirements will be laid upon
us.

In the case of those around us who are already Christians, we
must consider how to encourage them to grow in love and good
works (Heb. 10:24). We must reach out to our brothers and
sisters in Christ to edify, encourage, and motivate them to a
closer walk with the Lord and a more responsible life of stewardship before Him. By our own example, we can be a source of
much help and enrichment to our fellow believers. At the same
time, we will be able to benefit from their many gifts and talents.

In the case of those who are yet in their sins, we have a two-
fold responsibility. In the first place, we must exemplify the life-
style of those who are fully surrendered to Christ, showing forth
His love and truth in all the circumstances and relationships of
our lives. At the same time, we must look for opportunities to
share the gospel with those around us. We are as those who
stand on the watchtower, and we must warn those around us of

the dangers ahead if they fail to submit to the love of Christ (Isa. 62:6). We are, as Paul said, debtors to the lost. We owe it to them to share the gospel of Christ at every opportunity (Rom. 1:14–17).

5. *We must commit ourselves to discovering new and creative ways of accomplishing the work we have been given to do.* Creativity is the process of giving form and shape to the ideals, notions, goals, and aspirations by which we live in the world. And, as world changers, we have a great deal of raw material to spark our personal creativity.

Two key elements are necessary to the creative process. The first of these is encounter. By encounter we mean the heightening of our consciousness with respect to our world, our work, and the people around us. How well do we truly understand God's world-changing plans? How thoroughly acquainted are we with the various facets of our work? How well do we know the people with whom we work—their interests, skills, and aspirations? Only as we consciously and persistently work at broadening the horizons of our awareness concerning such matters as these can we hope to become more creative individuals.

Such encounters might take many forms. Certainly, continuing to grow in our understanding of the Christian world and life view is absolutely critical. We must commit ourselves to the reading, study, and discussion that will equip us to have a world changer's outlook on every aspect of human life and interest.

But there is more. How much do we know about the organizational structures within which we work? The field of endeavor of which we are a part? The work of others in this field? The equipment at our disposal and its capabilities? The background and potential of the people with whom we labor? New developments in technology or working procedure? In all these areas and many more there is room for us to grow in the area of our work in this world. We will become more creative as we consciously work to develop this ability.

The second element undergirding an effective creative process is absorption. By this we mean simply becoming totally immersed and wholly caught up in whatever task is at hand. In the process of absorption we draw on the broad range of our encounters to introduce new suggestions, innovative solutions and approaches to our work. Each task can become an all-absorbing challenge, tapping the fountain of our personal creativity to the fullest.

The creative process itself is quite distinct. There is a growing body of literature on this subject, which points to certain constantly recurring features of an effective creative strategy. Briefly, that process goes something like this: Faced with a new challenge or a difficult problem, we approach it with a great deal of intense concentration and hard work, seeking to apply traditional solutions as far as possible, yet in only a tentative manner. Content that we have exhausted the existing possibilities, we set the challenge aside and go into a period of rest. Here our mind totally leaves the specific problems we were addressing and floats freely over matters of a totally unrelated nature. This pattern of hard work and rest may be alternated for some time. Then suddenly, in a flash, an instant, the solution presents itself in rough design. The answer is clearly perceived, although only in outline form. Although it is a solution we have never considered, we perceive that it makes perfect sense. As we begin to think specifically about the solution, it becomes increasingly vivid, all the details falling clearly into place. Yet, it retains a brevity and a certainty that enables us to describe it concisely and enlist others in its realization.

This simple process has been testified to by great men and women from all ages and all walks of life. It can begin to characterize our approach to work more and more, according to how willing we are to commit ourselves to the encounter and absorption such a creative process requires. We want to take every thought captive to Christ and do all that we do so as to reflect the glory of God (2 Cor. 10:5; 1 Cor. 10:31). We will need every ounce of creativity we can muster if we are to succeed in this endeavor.

6. *We must commit ourselves to being satisfied with nothing less than excellence in our every endeavor.* At each stage of His creative work, God paused to reflect upon its perfection, pronouncing it "good" at each step along the way (cf. Gen. 1). We must pattern our work after that divine example. If we expect to hear God's "well done!" pronounced over the work of our hands, we will need to make certain as far as we are able that its quality is such as would elicit divine approval.

But how do we do that?

First, we must each one make certain that we do not have more to do than we can accomplish in an excellent manner. One of the regrettable characteristics of the Christian community is that 90 percent of the work is done by 10 percent of the people most of the time. As a result we are too easily satisfied with work that is shabby, incomplete, or mediocre at best, just so long as something gets done.

This is not what God wants of us. We must be selective in our work, doing only what is clearly within our priorities and capabilities and striving for excellence in all things. It would be vastly more desirable for today's world changer to do a few things well than a great many things in an incomplete or second-rate manner. We can be certain that those few things excellently done will receive the blessing of God and will endure.

Second, we must establish standards for our work. We must ask ourselves concerning our every task, "What would I want this job to look like or how would I want it to turn out if I knew Jesus were coming to inspect it and receive it unto Himself?" We must define our work standards in terms as specific as possible.

Having clearly defined standards will enable us to work consciously toward excellence. And the more we work consciously toward excellence, the more we can expect to achieve it.

Finally, we must pause for reflective evaluation of each stage of our work, measuring our accomplishments against the standards we have set. It will be helpful to have others involved with us in this process of evaluation. It will also be helpful if we have some objective instruments (forms, measurements, and so on) at our disposal, so that we do not simply have to rely on subjective opinion. Such periodic evaluations will enable us to stay on target toward excellence in all we do.

How Does Your Garden Grow?

How does *your* garden grow? Are you satisfied with the quality of your work? Is it fully pleasing to God and making a specific contribution to His purpose?

If we are truly going to change the world, we will have to apply ourselves to the task with all conscientiousness, zeal, and perseverance. Nothing short of an all-out effort on the part of each and every one of us will produce the desired results. We want men to see our good works and glorify our Father who is in heaven, and Jesus promised that we could expect this to happen (Matt. 5:16). By our example, as we let our "light so shine before men," we can show that work can truly have meaning and make a significant contribution of good toward the lives of others. And we can gain the attention of those around us for our Lord Jesus Christ and His world-changing way of life.

Questions for Study or Discussion

1. Make a list below of all the spheres or areas in which you are currently involved. Then list beside each area the *specific work* required of you.

Area   *Work*

2. Make a brief comment about the significance of each of the following verses for your work in each of the above areas.

1 Corinthians 10:31—

Ephesians 4:28—

Exodus 36:1—

1 Corinthians 4:1–2—

For Further Reading

Lockerbie, D. Bruce. *The Timeless Moment.* Westchester, Ill.: Cornerstone Books, 1980.

Rookmaaker, H. R. *The Creative Gift.* Westchester, Ill.: Cornerstone Books, 1981.

10

A Call to Oneness

"That They May Be One"

Jesus Christ must be set forth as the supreme and final answer for every human need.

Only Jesus Christ can take away the guilt that torments so many of the men and women of this generation. Only He can fill the gaps where love has all but disappeared. Only Jesus can give us the wisdom to anticipate and begin to address the multitude of needs arising on every hand. Only through the strength and love available in Jesus Christ can men and women find the power, purpose, and peace that can reduce the tensions, assuage the fears, and rekindle the hopes of this forlorn world.

As those who aspire to become the world changers of this age, we must ask ourselves, "How can we best help the world to understand the promise and fulfillment that can be experienced in Jesus Christ? How can we help them to believe that He has been sent to bring us the good things of God?"

Jesus Christ Himself has given us the key to reaching the world. In John 17:20–21 He makes it eminently plain and clear: "Neither pray I for these alone, but for them also which shall believe on me through their word; That they all may be one; as thou, Father, art in me, and I in thee, that they also may be one in us: that the world may believe that thou hast sent me."

Notice the result that Jesus has in mind here: "That the world may believe that thou hast sent me." He was interested in the same thing as we are, namely, helping the world to understand the Good News that He brings. Jesus knew that He was the only effective means of changing the world in any kind of positive and lasting way. But, if that was to happen, the world would have to come to the place where it began to believe that Jesus had been sent by God for their well-being. This is the central concern of His prayer. He is praying for the same thing that we have been praying and working for all this time.

Notice, second, who the focus of His prayer involves—not just His immediate disciples, "but for them also which shall believe on me through their word." His prayer concerns all those in every age who would come to faith in Christ as a result of the preaching and writing of the apostles. That includes each one of us! Jesus had us in mind as having some role in the world's coming to believe that God the Father had sent Him to men.

But precisely what is that role? How did Jesus perceive that we could play a part in the world's arrival at faith in Him, thus finding the wisdom, love, and power it would need to become totally and radically new?

The key is our oneness in Him and in one another.

"That they all may be one . . . that the world may believe that thou hast sent me." Jesus shows us in this prayer that the oneness of His people is an indispensable part of the world's coming to believe in Him. If the world—in all its sorrow, all its trouble, and all its pain—is ever to take seriously the soothing and saving message of God's love, it will be because they see a body of believers, demonstrating their oneness in Christ. The world is looking for living evidence that God's love can transform human lives. When that begins to happen, we can expect that the world will begin to listen more carefully to the message of Jesus we proclaim.

A Disappointing Situation

Yet, what does the world see as it looks about to survey the evidence of oneness in the Christian community in our day?

- Nearly 30,000 different denominations of believers, few, if any, having any fellowship, communion, or collaboration with one another
- Local churches intensely protective of their own memberships, frequently resorting to charges of "sheep stealing" toward other churches within the same city

- Church memberships riddled with petty quarreling, strifes, and divisions, so exhausted with their own struggles that they have no strength to reach out to their neighbors in love
- A vast and growing Christian community in the Western World that seems largely indifferent to the sufferings of its brothers and sisters in Christ in other lands

If there is but little indication that the world is taking our gospel more seriously in these turbulent times, the explanation may lie, at least in part, in our failure to produce a genuine demonstration of the oneness we possess in Christ. Jesus might just as easily have phrased His prayer in John 17 something like this: "I pray for those generations of Christians that are yet to come. Help them to be one. For the world, which needs so desperately to be changed, will never believe that You have sent Me unless it sees a oneness among Our people."

Clearly, then, if we are going to help the world begin to understand the message of Jesus Christ, we must pay more attention to this matter of our oneness in Him.

A Challenge for Each of Us

And here there is a challenge for each and every one of us. As those who know the importance of the gospel for the men and women of our generation, and as those who are determined to become the world changers of this age, we must both understand and accept our responsibility for bringing about the oneness that Jesus knew to be so important to His world-changing plan.

Only if we accept the central importance of our oneness in Christ, and only if we commit ourselves to doing everything within our power to establish and assert that oneness, can we expect that what Jesus foresaw will come to pass: The world will believe in Him.

The Basis of Our Oneness

Oneness in Christ, then, is the foundation from which we can begin to change the world.

What is the basis of our oneness in Christ? Over the years, believers have sought for a concept of oneness in many different areas. At first it was believed that a mere creedal statement could serve as a proper criterion for Christian oneness. In the early years of the church, councils of church leaders were often convened to deal with doctrinal matters so that those who were determined to be among the orthodox could have a creed of belief that would serve to unite them. Such canons as the Apostles' and Nicene Creeds arose out of this need to manifest Christian unity in the form of a common statement of faith.

In other ages of the church's history more bizarre and outlandish bases of unity were set forth. These included such matters as a common language, a particular political allegiance, opposition to this or that, a certain manner of dress, and even type of hair style! We look upon such criteria as but poor means of determining our oneness in Christ—but our age has its own absurdities when it comes to this area!

If we are to understand the common ground for our oneness in Christ, we shall have to look to the Word of God for the wisdom that only it can provide. Here we find that the only true basis for our oneness in Christ and in one another is in God Himself: "Endeavouring to keep the unity of the Spirit in the bond of peace. There is one body, and one Spirit, even as ye are called in one hope of your calling; One Lord, one Faith, one baptism, One God and Father of all, who is above all, and through all, and in you all" (Eph. 4:3-6).

Paul says that God Himself is the basis for our unity in Christ because only He is "above all." He is the only legitimate focus of our loyalty, our worship, and our adoration. He is above all. He invites, nay, *commands* us to keep our eyes on Him, lest we become sidetracked to lesser matters when it comes to our unity in Christ.

Further, He alone is "through all." It is God Himself who is to be expressed in the fruit of the Spirit, the tokens of love, and the exercise of Christian gifts by believers. He alone is to be seen as the One whose life is to be lived out through our own. Like Paul we must say that we have been crucified with Christ, living our lives in these times only by the power He generates within us. He becomes the purger of our sins, the source of our manifest goodness, and the power for our witness to Christ. We must look for and encourage in one another the living out of God's life through our own.

Finally, God is the only common possession of each and every believer. He is "in you all." Thus, we must look to Him as our source of strength for accepting others with all their faults, as well as for overcoming our own. We must find in God the common focus of our life together as members of the believing community.

We will not find our basis for oneness in any sort of creed or external criterion. As important as these may be in setting forth and demonstrating our faith before the watching world, they can never alone suffice for keeping the unity of the Spirit in the bond of peace. Only the insight, perception, power, grace, and commitment to one another that come from personally experiencing the God who is *above, through,* and *in* us all can enable us to begin to celebrate and to express the oneness we have in Christ.

The Means to Oneness

On this basis we shall then need an understanding of the means of our oneness that the Scriptures prescribe. How do we appropriate this basis of our oneness into our everyday lives?

The apostle Paul tells us that the first step toward maximizing our unity in Christ is for each of us to concentrate on developing a like-mindedness with our brothers and sisters in Christ. He calls us to "be likeminded, having the same love, being of one accord, of one mind" (Phil. 2:2).

Certainly there can be no outward demonstrations of our oneness in Christ without there first being present within each and every one of us a common outlook on life. Only as we concentrate on the things that we believe together can we expect that those common ideals will begin to generate a pattern of oneness in our life-styles.

Yet, it seems that it is precisely here that so many Christians begin to encounter difficulties. We are so prone to emphasize the things separating us as believers that we overlook what binds us together. We are unable to promote a oneness of mind because we are so busy extolling the particular virtues of our individual theological or ethical system over that of every other Christian on the block. Every denomination has its distinctives; every church has its peculiarities; every believer has his or her pet doctrine. What it all adds up to is a fragmented church, a community of believers who have more in common than any other group of people in the world, but who are nevertheless unable to get together with one another for any prolonged or significant undertaking.

Unless we can first develop a spirit of like-mindedness among ourselves, we can never hope to demonstrate the kind of oneness in Christ that will convince the watching world of the truth of His gospel.

This is not to suggest that theological distinctives do not have their place. It is only to insist that they must not be allowed to jeopardize or subvert our mission in Christ, which is to convince the world of its need for Him. If we can learn to concentrate more on the things that tend to accord, harmony, and agreement among us, we will be taking some giant steps toward cultivating an atmosphere of oneness within the Christian community. And this is the first step toward actualizing that divine basis under-girding our unity in Christ.

We must also be willing to undertake the hard work which will be necessary to make our oneness in Christ a reality. Paul says that in this effort we must "Let nothing be done through strife or vainglory . . . " (Phil. 2:3). That is, we must be certain that our motives are right in any cooperative venture we might undertake. We must make certain that we are calling attention to the glory of God and the unity of His people and not just to our magnanimity in initiating some concerted Christian activity.

Furthermore, we must "Look not every man on his own things, but every man also on the things of others" (Phil. 2:4). We will have vastly more success in our common endeavors as believers if we are careful to focus our efforts on the needs of others more than on ourselves. Here there are excellent opportunities for Christians to work together toward the alleviation of particular needs within their communities. As churches set aside their own programs to collaborate with one another in address-ing needs within their communities, they will make eminently visible the oneness they are coming to possess in their relation-ships with one another.

The important thing is to begin planning and looking for op-portunities to make our unity in Christ visible through collabo-rative effort of one kind or another. Maybe we will begin in a common service of worship. Perhaps it will be in a joint evange-listic outreach in our city. It can be any of a hundred and one different ways of showing the watching world that we are one in

Christ and that this oneness enables us to accomplish more together than we ever could alone.

Finally, we must follow the example of Christ in seeing prayer as a critical means of bringing our oneness to fruition. As He prayed in Gethsemane for us to be one, so let us pray for one another. Let pastors meet together for prayer for one another, their churches, their communities, and the world. Let churches set apart a portion of their worship time for praying for the other churches in their city. And let individual believers learn to meet together for prayer in interdenominational and interchurch groups in homes all across the face of our land. Such prayer will be a powerful means of our beginning to make real the oneness we have in Christ.

The Scope of Our Oneness

But just how broad is the scope of our oneness? What are the limits of its reach? Without addressing this question, we will never be able to know whether or not we are realizing the fullness of the benefits or the potential of our unity in Christ.

The answer to this question lies in three important directions.

First, our oneness transcends all interpersonal differences that might exist between individual believers. We must come to see that what we have together in Jesus Christ is greater than anything which might drive us apart. Whether our oneness is threatened by matters doctrinal, relational, or of any other kind, we can learn to draw on the God who is above, through, and in us all to give us the strength to let our unity in Him preserve a spirit of fellowship and peace among us. *But this must be the constant and conscious effort of every believer.* We must strive to keep our oneness intact so that our testimony to the living Christ will have the credibility it deserves.

Second, we have already indicated that our oneness in Christ must be allowed to transcend all ecclesiastical boundaries. This includes relationships between Christ-honoring churches, denominations, and Christian organizations of all kinds.

We can only imagine what the impact might be in cities all across America if the churches of the land would agree to cooperate and collaborate on just one project of community concern. Maybe it could be the creation of a job-training program, a community thrift store, a rural co-op, a program for adult literacy training, or any of a score of other possibilities. What grand opportunities for working together present themselves to us in a day! Certainly the skeptics in our midst would have cause to reconsider their attitudes toward Christian faith should such joint ventures begin to be seen.

Or what might be the result if whole denominations were to pool their resources to address some urgent national need? And what if every missionary and evangelistic organization could sit down regularly to strategize and encourage one another? We can certainly believe that vastly more would be accomplished for the glory of Christ and the advancement of His kingdom than we have thus far dared to dream.

But there is one more aspect of the scope of our oneness that presents unique and urgent opportunities for us to begin actualizing what we already possess in Jesus Christ. This has to do with the international dimension of our oneness.

In the Apostles' Creed we profess to believe in the one "catholic church." By this we mean the church in its universality as a body spanning every culture, every language, and every type of national distinctive. As a people, Christians are one in Him across any geographical and cultural boundaries that might separate them.

In our day this is an aspect of our oneness that cries out for recognition. In other lands our brothers and sisters in Christ are routinely imprisoned, harassed, and tortured for their faith. Their only "crime" is believing the gospel. They refuse to submit to the mandates of tyrants who are determined to make atheism the official religion of the state. Yet, we in the West remain largely indifferent to their plight and are silent in the face of numerous opportunities to protest and to proclaim our oneness in Christ. We do not cry out in agony as our own government persists in feeding and equipping the tormentors of our brethren. We make little or no effort to provide those suffering brethren with any encouragement or hope. They almost never enter into our prayers.

Yet, even across the iron curtains and concrete walls of ruthless oppressors, these are *our* people, men and women who have more in common with us than many of the people we see in our neighborhoods and places of work each and every day. One day we will look those beleaguered brothers and sisters in the eye. Then we will understand with perfect clarity what we scarcely ever think about now: These are our brethren in Christ, and they await our reaching out to make manifest the oneness with them that God has given us.

It is never too late to begin working toward showing forth the unity we have in Jesus Christ. And it is certain that our efforts to change the world will continue to lack a most fundamental and powerful dimension so long as our oneness in Christ is nothing more than a mere theological concept. It is time to begin doing something about our unity in Christ. It is time for a general call to oneness on the part of believers everywhere.

"By this shall all men know that ye are my disciples, if ye have love one to another . . . . That they may all be one . . . that the world may believe that thou has sent me" (John 13:35; 17:21). With such a mandate and such a promise to guide us, how can we fail to heed the call to oneness, which issues forth out of the very depths of our being?

Questions for Study or Discussion

1. How does Paul express the unity amid diversity of our oneness in Christ in 1 Corinthians 12?

2. What was Paul's attitude toward the kind of factionalism that jeopardizes our unity in Christ (1 Corinthians 1:10–13)?

3. What barriers to Christian oneness exist in your own life today?

For Further Reading

Banks, Robert. *Paul's Idea of Community.* Grand Rapids, Mich.: Wm. B. Eerdmans Publishing Co., 1980.

Moore, T. M. *Belonging to One Another.* Evangelism Explosion, P.O. Box 23820, Fort Lauderdale, FL 33307.

Schaeffer, Francis A. *The Church at the End of the Twentieth Century.* Downers Grove, Ill.: IVP, 1970.

Snyder, Howard A. *The Community of the King.* Downers Grove, Ill.: IVP, 1978.

11

Thy Kingdom Come

Great and Precious Promises

"Call unto me, and I will answer thee, and shew thee great and mighty things, which thou knowest not" (Jer. 33:3).

With such an astounding promise set before us, there can be only one explanation for the Christian community's inability, so far, to change the world in any more powerful and comprehensive a manner than is presently in evidence. We simply have not asked!

The apostle Paul tells us that our God "is able to do exceeding abundantly above all that we ask or think" (Eph. 3:20). Why is it, then, that this exceeding abundance has not yet been brought to pass in our midst and in the lives of people everywhere? ". . . ye have not, because ye ask not" (James 4:2).

Jesus told us, "And all things, whatsoever ye shall ask in prayer, believing, ye shall receive" (Matt. 21:22). Why is it, then, that the "all things" we have been promised from the Father's bounty are not the present possession of His people? *It can only be that we have not asked.*

We can talk of changing the world, hope for it, and long for it with all our being. We can lay out careful and comprehensive plans, devise long- and short-range strategies, and organize movements from coast to coast. We can raise money, publish manuscripts, and circulate petitions. We can shout, "We've had enough!" until our throats are hoarse, and we can commit our energies, our resources, and our resolve to changing the world for the honor and glory of Jesus Christ.

Yet, if we do not pray, if we do not look earnestly to God in daily and moment-by-moment prayer, we cannot expect to succeed in any kind of lasting manner.

The Starting Point

Prayer must be the starting point for changing the world. In prayer we acknowledge our Father's superintending grace over all the affairs of men. In prayer we confess our dependence upon Him for all our hopes and needs. In prayer we find the strength to fulfill our individual callings to serve the Lord, and in prayer we focus on the vision of what God intends to bring to pass, beseeching Him to perform His will in our midst.

Clearly, therefore, if we are truly serious about changing the world, we may not neglect the ministry of prayer.

Like disciples of long ago, we need to come to the Lord saying, "Lord, teach us to pray" (Luke 11:1). And we need to consider carefully once again the response that we might most reasonably expect to hear from His mouth: "After this manner therefore pray . . ." (Matt. 6:9).

The Model Prayer

The Lord's Prayer holds the key to our success in being able to change the world. By understanding and putting into practice the guidelines for prayer that Jesus Himself has set forth, we can be assured of victory in our struggles to change the world. That Jesus laid great emphasis on the role of prayer in the life of faith goes without saying. That we need to reconsider our prayer lives and recommit ourselves to what He taught concerning this most important subject seems to be clearly indicated.

The Lord's Prayer is intended to be a guide for us in seeking the Father's will for our lives. Jesus said, "After this manner therefore pray ye . . ." (Matt. 6:9). The prayer He then offered, as majestic and beautiful as it is in and of itself, is primarily intended to provide us with some contours for our own praying. It gives us understanding into the proper mood for our prayers and tells us of the proper focus for our prayers. It reminds us of the arena and the scope within which our prayers are to find their realization. We can discover new power in our praying if we will let this prayer of Jesus teach us how we ought to pray. And, with new power in our praying, we will be better able to believe God for all the promises He has determined to bring to pass for His people. Those promises hold the hope for a changed world. Through powerful prayer, they can begin to be realized in our lives.

The Proper Mood

Let us look first of all, then, at the words Jesus taught us to follow as indicating the proper mood for our prayers: *Hallowed be Thy name.*

Prayer is conversation set aside for God. It is the communication flowing from us to Him as we lay bare the concerns and desires of our hearts. From the first words of our prayer, we want to make certain that those cares and aspirations are properly presented, as being surrendered to God for His gracious and wise attention, rather than merely submitted in the form of some sort of personal "wish list."

This petition—*Hallowed be Thy name*—can help us remember to approach our prayer life in the proper frame of mind. Although it is to our loving and most kind heavenly Father that we come, we must yet bear in mind that He is seated on His throne of grace (Heb. 4:16). And though we may come boldly before that hallowed throne, we come nevertheless as those who freely acknowledge the great gulf which separates us from our gracious and holy God. We are but poor sinners in His presence. Yet, the way to His throne has been cleared for us by Jesus Christ our Lord. By His mercy we are made clean; yet we dare not presume upon that mercy nor comfort ourselves in prayer as though we ourselves had somehow been able to accomplish our own redemption.

Hallowed be Thy name. He is the God who is high and lifted up, whose beginnings are without telling, whose goings forth are of old, whose ends are never to be seen. He is the Creator, the Sovereign Lord, the infinite and all-wise God of heaven and earth. He knows the creation intimately throughout, from the most minute particle of the atom to the most immense galaxy of the great cosmos. He holds them all in His mighty hand, together with each and every one of us. Were He for a moment to withdraw His sustaining power from underneath the framework of the universe, the whole of it would evaporate into mere nothingness in less than the span of a moment. He is the Lord and there is none other. He is the alone and almighty Most Holy One. He is the altogether unique and hallowed One God, far beyond the scrutiny of any mere mortal or other created being. He is God over all, set apart by Himself without rival or peer. He is the One alone whose name is truly hallowed. And He is our Father—our Father whom we may approach in prayer. He eagerly anticipates the petitions of our hearts.

Our Aspirations

Thy kingdom come. I do not believe there is any more succinct way of expressing our world-changing aspirations than this— *Thy kingdom come.* In order to understand what we mean by this, it will be necessary to make certain that we know what the kingdom of God is and what we are being instructed to pray for concerning that kingdom.

Jesus used the terms "kingdom of God" and "kingdom of heaven" in a wide variety of instances during His public ministry. The terms are actually interchangeable and were meant by our Lord to focus our attention on the scope and power of the reign of God over the affairs of men and the universe. Quite simply put, the kingdom of God is the place where God reigns in power. There is one sense in which we must acknowledge that this reign of God is already in place in our midst. Jesus taught that His ability to cast out devils was clear evidence of the fact that the kingdom of God had come to men (Matt. 12:28). He even taught us to understand that the kingdom could operate within our own lives (Luke 17:21), so that God could change men by His ruling power from the inside out, as we have previously stated.

Thus, we are to pray that this kingdom, which even now is subduing the hearts and lives of men and women everywhere, might more fully and forcefully come in our own time. Jesus teaches us earnestly to pray that the reign of God might be more and more in evidence in the lives of the people of our world.

Here it is good that we ask ourselves: Would Jesus teach us to pray for something that He did not fully intend to bring to pass in our midst? Or, looked at in another way, would He instruct us to pray for something which He knew full well He was determined to frustrate?

Hardly.

In teaching us to pray that the kingdom of God would come in power in our lives and in the lives of our friends, our neighbors, those who govern our land, those who hold positions of prominence in institutions all over the world, and countless others besides, *Jesus is calling us to an act of faith by which we can have a vital and powerful role in changing our world.* We express our faith in Him and in our heavenly Father's powerful ability to bring in His kingdom when we pray pointedly and specifically for the people we know who need to be a focus of that kingdom's power today. No wonder Paul taught us to pray for kings and governors and all who are in authority over us. He knew such prayers could make a difference. No wonder we are instructed to pray for one another. Such prayer can provide a powerful support for our lives. Prayer that God's power and His kingdom might be realized "within us" is a guaranteed way of changing things so that they might begin to be more in conformity with the will of God.

We must also bear in mind that the kingdom of God is something that is yet to come. It is among us, but it is not yet here in all its fullness. Although that situation will only come about at the return of our Lord Jesus Christ in power to set up His eternal kingdom in the new heavens and the new earth, we must pray equally fervently for this to occur: "Even so, come, Lord Jesus" (Rev. 22:20).

Thus, we must permit this first word of instruction concerning the petitions of our prayers to focus those prayers on the areas and individuals of our world where the need is greatest for the powerful exercise of God's reigning might. And we are to pray earnestly for the hastening of that day when Jesus Himself will return to wipe away every tear and banish the darkness once and for all.

The Will of God

Thy will be done. This petition follows directly on the former. Concerning the bringing in of God's reign in our midst, we would have it effect His will among us.

But what is God's will? And how can we pray for it?

Well, let us consider some rather basic questions: Is it God's will that men murder one another? Steal from one another? Lie to and deceive one another? Slander one another? Is it God's will that homes be torn apart by adultery or strife? That righteousness be shelved in favor of personal whim? That the Great Commission be neglected or ignored by the churches of the world?

Of course not. We recognize each of these conditions to be directly contrary to some clear statement of the Scriptures, which we know to be the will of God. Thus, we may begin to pray specifically that the will of God, as it has been clearly set forth in the Bible, may come to pass in the affairs of men and nations. Moreover, we can be quite bold and specific in our prayers for this.

There are, of course, many areas in which the will of God is not so clear. Yet, following the advice of James, we may commit our thinking, planning, preparations, and daily affairs to prayer for the will of God to be fulfilled in whatsoever we do (James 4:13–15).

Jesus further teaches us concerning this petition that we ought to pray for the accomplishing of God's will *on earth, as it is in heaven.* That is, we want to see God's will brought to pass among men as it is among the heavenly hosts—willingly, freely, gladly, and out of loving obedience to the directives of our Father in heaven. If this is to happen, those of us who understand and know the Savior are going to have to willingly, freely, gladly, and obediently reach out to the lost men and women of this age with the Good News of Jesus' love. Only thus will their hearts ever be prepared to submit in joyful obedience to the will of God for their lives.

Again, we must believe that in teaching us to pray in this manner, Jesus is fully able and willing to grant our requests. We must believe that our fervent and sincere prayers for the will of God to come to pass on earth will not fall on deaf ears in the courts of heaven. We must pray specifically, confidently, boldly, gladly, and in eager anticipation of the results we desire. But we must also be certain that as good stewards of the kingdom and of God's will, we are faithfully working to bring His will to pass in our own lives. Effectual prayer requires us to be diligent and circumspect concerning our own lives at the same time that we call upon God for the lives of others.

Our Daily Bread

Give us this day our daily bread. The Lord Jesus knew that the will of God is designed so as to be brought to pass on earth primarily through the instrumentality of His people. In many periods of human history and in the lives of many individuals, God has worked through extraordinary means of circumstance and situation to bring His will to pass. Yet, His work on earth is primarily meant to be done by men and women who have willingly aligned themselves with Him.

Thus, when we beseech God to bring His will to pass "on earth, as it is in heaven," we must bear in mind that we are, in a very real sense, requesting of Him our own marching orders for the battles ahead. For, if we are to succeed in the calling that our heavenly Father has prepared for us, we will require strengths and abilities not inherently our own.

Embedded in this request for "our daily bread" is a petition for the daily necessities we must have if we are to succeed as people through whom God will bring His will to pass among men.

For example, if we ask God to fulfill His will in the life of a particular loved one—perhaps by that individual's becoming a Christian—then we must also pray for the wherewithal and opportunity to be used of God in seeing that happy result come to pass.

If it is a part of our daily prayer that God would rid our society of such evils as abortion, homosexuality, and corruption, then we must also include in our petitions a request for the strength, ability, wisdom, and opportunity to be used by Him in playing a part in the eradication of such blights.

If we are wont to pray that God would take the gospel to the farthest corners of the globe, then we must also pray that He would supply us with the ability to have a part in that important task—either by going ourselves, or by giving so that others may go in our place.

The petition that God would supply our daily bread is vastly more than the mere setting before Him of our personal wants and needs. Not until we have come to see this request as inseparably linked to the one that has gone before, will we begin to understand its proper meaning. What *we* earnestly beseech God to do in the bringing to pass of His will on earth, *He* is determined to accomplish through human vessels. Let us make certain in our prayers that our hearts, minds, and spirits are as eager to be involved in realizing the will of God as in requesting it.

Forgiveness

Forgive us our debts. We cannot begin to stress enough the importance of this petition. There are two aspects of this prayer that are important to bear in mind.

The first has to do with its benefit in keeping us mindful of who we are and what we are inclined to do. It can be said of even the best of us that we are the most miserable of sinners. We are inclined to do evil and apt to fall into sin whenever we become careless of our tendencies or when left unto ourselves. This gentle reminding ourselves in prayer of our sinfulness can have the effect of keeping us both close to the Father and circumspect about our own lives. As we are reminded of our sinful nature, we will become more and more prone to turn to God in prayer in times of need. Also, we will be more careful about the kinds of influences and activities we allow to become part of our lives.

Second, since it is inevitable that we will fall into sin from time to time, this petition can also have the effect of cleansing us and once again rightly restoring us to our place of fellowship with the Father. We have the blessed assurance that if we will confess our sins, He will be faithful and just to forgive them and to cleanse us of all unrighteousness (1 John 1:9). We must learn to rely on this promise and to come contritely to God as His Spirit calls us to confess our sins before Him.

None of our prayers will be of any value so long as unconfessed sin lingers in our lives (Isa. 59:2). Moreover, we will not be inclined to confess our sins if we continuously fail to bear in mind our imperfect and sin-prone condition. Thus, this petition is of great importance for those who would have a powerful prayer life. Let us learn to pray it faithfully, sincerely, and consistently.

Deliverance from Evil

Lead us not into temptation, but deliver us from evil. In this final petition, two absolutely critical aspects of the struggle for a changed world come into focus. Both of them, moreover, are focused on us.

First is acknowledgment that evil is a very real and active presence in today's world. Satan is no mere fairy tale. He is a real being, supported by equally real and evil beings, which together seek the frustration of God's purposes and the destruction of our lives (1 Pet. 5:8; Eph. 6:12). Although it is true that one of our greatest faults can be the tendency to overestimate and overdramatize the powers and wiles of the devil, it is equally dangerous to underestimate them and thus be unprepared to recognize and deal with them when they present themselves.

The proper place to begin equipping ourselves to handle the devil is in prayer. For in prayer we can ask the Father to so prepare our way as to keep us from falling unwittingly into the hands of the adversary. Without such preparation, we are, as they say, "fair game."

The second critical aspect of our struggle that this petition highlights is the absolute sovereignty of God. Certainly, there could be no more fitting place to remind ourselves of this glorious truth than in prayer.

We have just implored the bringing in of God's will among the men and nations of our day. We have made ourselves available and sought the wherewithal we will need in order to see that request come to fruition. Yet, we have acknowledged that we are but fragile vessels against a powerful adversary who seeks to destroy our hopes and our lives. Truly, it would seem, if our prayers are to bear any fruit, it will only be as the sovereign God of heaven and earth intervenes to guide and protect us as He works out His will in and through us.

As we pray, "Lead us not into temptation," we put both ourselves and the forces arrayed against us in a proper perspective. Seen in this light, all fear, distress, and doubt are banished. We are in the hands of a powerful and sovereign God. There is nothing to fear, for He will not suffer us to be tempted above what we are able to bear (1 Cor. 10:13). He will deliver us and keep us because He is able (2 Tim. 1:12). Truly, it is good to remind ourselves of this, in the light of all that we shall have prayed before.

A Hymn of Praise

Can it be any wonder that this great exemplary prayer should end in a hymn of praise? *For Thine is the kingdom, and the power, and the glory forever!* Certainly there is no credit that can be expected to accumulate to us in the carrying out of God's will according to our prayers. Only *He* is worthy of praise, and only they will be trusted to be the actors in His eternal redemptive plan who know how to focus all praise and attention on Him. Let us exercise ourselves to that end in our prayers.

What a release, what an exhilaration, what a thrill to sing the matchless praises of our God! What freedom, what joy, and what strength accrue to those who learn thus to sing! And what power is released within us when we show that we are no usurpers of the Father's glory, but rather acknowledge that we are His faithful children and servants, seeking only and above all else that His marvelous glory be declared! Let us sing His praises daily, and let us look for Him to use us as faithful stewards in the accomplishment of His glorious purposes among men.

Praying the Lord's Prayer

But how can we learn to begin praying like this? Alas, for many the Lord's Prayer has become little more than a merely verbal exercise, a muttering of phrases and lines with no thought taken for the power that could be unleashed.

Many have found it helpful to let this prayer serve its intended function, as a general guide to their own prayers. You, too, might find it powerful in this way. Begin by praying the first line, "Our Father, which art in heaven." Then pause and let your spirit wander over that address. Recall that gracious act by which God became your Father. Thank Him for it and for the Lord Jesus Christ. Think upon the tender mercies by which He shows Himself to be a loving Father to you. Recall them out loud with a word of thanks at each item. Meditate on heaven, think about the beauties around the throne where your Father dwells, and thank Him for the mansion that is even now being prepared for you. Recall the joys that are at His right hand forevermore. Rejoice to think that you have an eternal share in these wonders.

Praise and adore your Father for the hallowedness of His name. Then begin to make specific mention of the matters concerning His kingdom and will that are on your heart. Pray for specific people, particular needs, and the stated requests of others. Ask Him for the opportunity and strength to be used in realizing these requests. Then go through the rest of this prayer in like manner, praying the petition Christ taught and pausing to reflect and pray more specifically over whatsoever matters the Spirit brings to your mind. End with a hymn of praise, perhaps a song such as "Praise to the Lord, the Almighty, the King of Creation" or "Praise Him, Praise Him, Jesus, our Blessed Redeemer." Then go forth in total expectancy of new found strength, heightened power, and added opportunities to be used in a world-changing way by God.

What would be the effect in your life if you could actually begin to pray regularly in the way Christ taught? How would your life be changed, and how could your changed life begin to have an impact on the people around you? Consider what would happen if all God's people everywhere began so to pray. Undoubtedly, we would unleash a world-changing tide across the face of the earth, which could roll back the flood of humanism, inundate and eliminate the march of Marxism, and usher in a new age of freedom and life for the men and women of this generation!

The secret of any and all our success will begin only in prayer. Are we up to it? "Call unto me, and I will answer thee, and shew thee great and mighty things, which thou knowest not" (Jer. 33:3).

Questions for Study or Discussion

1. What are some of the hindrances to an effective prayer life that you have encountered?

2. What are some effective helps to prayer that you have learned to use?

3. What do each of the following verses suggest about what constitutes an effective prayer life?

Philippians 1:3—

1 Thessalonians 5.17—

Philippians 4:6—

James 5:16—

Luke 18:1—

For Further Reading

Bounds, E. M. *Power Through Prayer.* Grand Rapids, Mich.: Baker Books, 1977.
Moore, T. M. *"Call Unto Me ... and I Will Answer."* Evangelism Explosion, P. O. Box 23820, Fort Lauderdale, FL 33307.

12

From Glory to Glory

A Generation of World Changers

In many ways Jesus sought to make it clear that His intention for His people was that they should be a generation of world changers. He said they were the "salt of the earth" (Matt. 5:13), the preservative of everything good and decent among men. He called them "a city that is set on a hill" (Matt. 5:14), a mighty fortress presiding over the affairs of men and nations. He said they were the "light of the world" (Matt. 5:14), pointing the way to faith, hope, and life in a sin-darkened world.

Jesus also likened His kingdom and its citizens to leaven worked into loaves of bread, spreading its good influence throughout (Matt. 13:33). He taught that they would become like the mustard plant, which provides food and shelter for a variety of living creatures (Matt. 13:31–32). And He commanded them to go and make all the nations disciples of the living and reigning Lord, followers of the greatest name and the greatest cause that could ever be (Matt. 28:18–20).

Can there be any doubt that the Lord Jesus intended that His people should become a dominant influence for goodness and truth in their generations? And can there be any doubt that this expectation is held forth for our generation as well?

Thus, to set our sights on becoming anything less than a generation of true world changers is to fail to adopt the vision that Jesus Himself spelled out for us, His people. It is to fall short of His expectations for us.

We must set ourselves to the task of changing our world in these troubled times, although it must be admitted that this is no light task.

Before us lies the greatest challenge that any people could encounter. Each of us as an individual believer must ponder the significance of this challenge for his or her own life. And together we must begin to envision what this awesome challenge portends for us as a worldwide community of those who have heeded the call of Jesus Christ.

A Unifying Vision

It will greatly help us in this challenge if we can adopt a unifying vision of what we are individually called to become as God's world changers. Throughout the Bible, it is characteristic of the Lord to lead His people into and through great challenges. He places before them a vision of the possibilities both of what they could become and what they could expect Him to achieve through them. We must seek out such a vision for ourselves.

We would submit that there could be no greater vision to motivate us into our world-changing task than that of the Lord Jesus Christ Himself. Truly, Jesus was the greatest world changer who ever lived. There has never been another like Him for having a profound influence for good on both history and the world.

No one has ever had more effect on the course of history and the ongoing events and interests of men and nations than has "the carpenter's son" from Nazareth.

No name has ever given rise to more noble intentions, endeavors, and institutions than that of Jesus.

No person has brought so much comfort, such high hope and supportive encouragement, to men and women from all walks of life, all nations, and all times as He.

Truly, Jesus Christ is the quintessential world changer. If we can isolate and concentrate on the particulars of His world-changing way of life, we can become more and more like Him. The apostle Paul advised us that as we behold the glory of our Lord Jesus reflected in the glass of God's Word, we can expect to be "changed into the same image from glory to glory, even by

the Spirit of the Lord" (2 Cor. 3:18). That is, the more we contemplate the image of Jesus Christ and the more we take His
person and His attributes into the context of our own self-
understanding, the more we will begin to see ourselves take on
that same image in our own lives.

We must set ourselves to the task of understanding the world-
changing example of the Lord Jesus, so that we might become
more like Him.

The Example of Christ

Let us, then, consider some of the particulars of the life and
work of the Lord Jesus in the light of what we have described as
the world-changing task confronting us today.

We have said that today's world changers would need a solid
foundation of the Word of God on which to take their stand.
Certainly, it was true of Jesus that He stood squarely on the
Word of God in all that He said and did. The apostle John tells
us, in fact, that Jesus *was* the very Word of God Himself, the
incarnate representation of the perfect will of God (John 1:1,
14). So perfectly did the person and life of Jesus Christ fulfill the
requirements and teachings of God's law that it could only be
true of Him that He was the Word of God. Jesus said that the
words He spoke were both Spirit and life (John 6:63). So thoroughly involved with the Word of God was Jesus that He could
identify with confidence His own teachings with those of the
Spirit and the Father. The Book of Hebrews tells us that Jesus
was so thoroughly the Word of God that through Him the Father has spoken to His people in these latter days (Heb. 1:1–2).

Thus, the example of Jesus is that our lives must be wholly
given over to the Word of God if we are to be the world changers He intends for us to be. We have on our own neither the
wisdom nor the strength to fulfill that which is required of us in
these days. Unless we find, as Jesus found, that we do not live by
bread alone but by every word that proceeds from the mouth of
God, we cannot expect to succeed in our world-changing task
(Matt. 4:4).

How is it with you when it comes to the Word of God? How
serious is your daily effort to understand the depths of its mysteries and truths? How faithfully do you strive to incorporate

into your own life the teachings that the Spirit of God presents for your understanding each and every day in His Word? And how ready are you to have the Word of God cast its light into every corner of your life and upon every aspect of your daily responsibilities and interests?

We cannot rise to become a generation of true world changers without a deepening understanding of and commitment to the Word of God. Let us, like Jesus Himself, endeavor to become so totally dedicated to and involved with the Word of God in the Bible that it takes over the whole of our lives and impels us into our daily tasks as mighty world changers for God.

We have also said that they who would change our world must be committed to the task of taking the gospel of Jesus Christ to all men. Certainly, Jesus Himself is the perfect model for how we ought to accomplish this.

Jesus bore witness to the kingdom of God on every occasion. Whether on hillsides, in taverns, in the homes of His friends as well as His enemies, before the sick and lowly, and before the rich and powerful, in the cities and in the countrysides, Jesus was ever prepared to talk about that great mission on which He had been sent.

And, in the same way that the Father sent Him, Jesus has sent us (John 20:21). How ready are we to speak a word of witness concerning the risen Lord Jesus Christ? When was the last time that you assayed to speak in the name of Jesus a word of hope that included the message of the gospel?

We will not change the world if we do not see the need for changing it from the inside out. Since only the gospel can bring the radical life changes all men and women need, we must commit ourselves to being bold and aggressive, sensitive and love-driven communicators of the gospel of God, even as was Jesus. We must be willing to share the Good News at all times and in all seasons, always taking into account the needs of the hearers and the level of their ability to understand what we would have them know (2 Tim. 4:2; 1 Cor. 9:22). Without such a commitment, we will surely fail in our world-changing undertakings.

We must also come to see that in Jesus we have the perfect example of how our homes can be changed unto the glory of God. Jesus showed a concern for homes and families throughout the course of His earthly ministry. Such compassion did He feel

for Jairus and his wife that He walked no small distance to
restore their daughter to them (Luke 8:41–56). Often He would
resort to the home of Mary and Martha, there to enjoy the
hospitality of loving sisters and their brother, there as well to
remind at least one of them of the central place the Word of
God must have in the homes of His people (Luke 10:38–42).
The apostle Paul tells us to consider Jesus as the head of our
homes, by Him to find the love and mutual submission to one
another that we must have as believers (Eph. 5:21–33).

Seeing Jesus move about the homes of Israel in His day, and
observing His presence in the homes of His people today, can
provide us with a new vision of what the family can become.

A changed world will come about only as each of us fulfills his
or her personal role as an economist of God, a faithful steward
over the gifts, possessions, time, and talents that we have been
given. Again Jesus provides us with a perfect example of how
God's economists must both understand and go about accomplishing their tasks.

Throughout the course of His earthly ministry, Jesus main-
tained a commitment to fulfilling the will of God in His life.
That is, Jesus determined to use all His talents, all His time, and
all His energies for the fulfillment of what He had come to know
as the Father's plan for His life. He had no time for lesser commitments and was unwilling to dissipate His strength or His
talents in the pursuit of frivolous endeavors. Jesus was, as we
say, "sold out" to the will of God for the whole of His life.

Jesus said that He did not seek His own will but that of the
Father who sent Him (John 5:30). This remained true even unto
the final hours of His earthly life (John 6:38–40; Mark 14:36).
Without such a commitment, we can imagine that the tempta-
tions and opportunities at every hand might have drawn Jesus
away from that which He had come to accomplish. Yet, such
was not the case.

Could He teach with power? Jesus determined to teach the
kingdom of God. Did He have any possessions? He resolved to
have no more than would be necessary for His kingdom task.
Did Jesus attract friends unto Himself? He made certain that
His relationships with them were directed toward the purposes
of God. Did Jesus recognize His obligations as a citizen, a son of
His mother, and a member of the kingdom community of God?

He fulfilled them all, always with a clear eye toward what would conduce to the glory of God in each instance.

Jesus was truly the Great Steward, God's Economist par excellence. As we contemplate His going about to fulfill His earthly tasks, let us look to see how carefully and faithfully He discharged them all to the greater glory of God. His example can motivate and give guidance to us.

We have said that a changed world would require a proper understanding of the role of government and a determination to ensure that civil authorities in our world abide by the guidelines of God's Word. Before we can expect governments to fulfill all that is required of them, we must first make certain that we are adequately self-governed by God's Word. We must be committed to fulfilling our role as citizens according to those same principles of moral discipline.

And, once again, Jesus can be seen as the supreme example of the self-governed man. He can show us the way to overcoming temptation. He can teach us how we ought to persist in the right course, regardless of the moral shortcuts or compromises that present themselves for our consideration.

Three times the devil sought to derail Jesus from His course of self-government by the Word of God. Three times he failed (Matt. 4:1-11). Jesus was able to stand boldly before the powers of His day because he was confident of His personal morality. He was confident that He had kept the will of God in His own life and was thus fully competent to speak the Word of God to the rulers and princes of His day. Without such a conviction of self-discipline, we cannot expect our governments to abide by the guidelines of God. By concentrating on the example of Jesus Christ, we can find the wisdom and strength required for moral government and its citizenry.

We also see in Jesus the Master Teacher who can show us how to fulfill our educational responsibilities. Jesus was the Master Teacher in that He was able to fit His instruction to children as well as to adults. He taught profound mysteries and propositional truths in simple and alluring ways. He used the common things of life—birds, farms, fish, coins, bread, cloth—to teach the most profound lessons men and women had ever heard. And, as a result, Jesus was able to make education both extremely interesting and eminently practical for those who followed Him.

Each of us bears responsibility for the education of others. We must ask ourselves before God what we can do to see to it that His truth is set forth accurately, powerfully, and with a perspective that will change men and women in our society. As we contemplate the teaching ministry of Jesus Christ, we can gain new insights into how we should proceed to fulfill our educational responsibilities.

We have also said that our world requires a new vision of the workplace and of how men and women ought to relate to one another therein. Again, Jesus can provide us with an ideal toward which we can aspire in our world-changing efforts.

Jesus taught us that our work must be seen as the work of God. Only then can we have the assurance that His blessings will be upon us in all that we do (John 9:4). We must expect that God can use our work in mighty ways to bring glory to Himself, so long as we seek faithfully to refer all that we do in the workplace to our Father in heaven. Jesus said, ". . . the works that I do shall [the believer] do also; and greater works than these shall he do" (John 14:12). Do we believe this? Are we convinced that our work can usher in the same world-changing results that followed the works of Jesus?

We must contemplate the work of Christ and seek to reach an understanding of our own work as somehow continuous with His. We will find that God will honor our labors for His purposes. We will see that even the work of our hands, as well as the work of our minds, can be used by God to change our world. Jesus, the Master Workman, has promised it.

Further, we have said that the world requires a living example of people united in a common venture. We must be a people striving to show our common bonds of love and fellowship and our dedication to common convictions and concerns, if our message is to be heeded. Here again, Jesus shows us the supreme example of how that unity ought to be expressed.

Because He is perfect God, Jesus was able to maintain an unbroken fellowship with the Father. Through prayer, faith, and obedience, Jesus showed what a life of oneness with God could accomplish among men. His careful circumspection over the affairs of His life, in the light of His relationship with His heavenly Father, remains an example for us of how our unity with God ought to be expressed.

Yet, by virtue of His being perfect man as well, Jesus is able to show us how to develop unity with one another. He became like us, identifying with our greatest weaknesses, feeling our greatest needs and deepest desires, so that, for us, He could show the way to salvation, faith, and life. By His example, we are summoned to a walk of consideration, sympathy, and mutual concern both for our brethren in Christ and for those in the world at large. Our union with God and with one another will flow naturally out of our relationships as we concentrate on the example of Christ and seek to make that pattern a reality in our own lives.

We can also see in Jesus the perfect model of the powerful life of prayer. Jesus always turned to prayer concerning the decisions and events of His life. He could be seen resorting to prayer in the morning and in the evening, in private and in public.

In John 17 we have a beautiful example of the heartfelt prayers of our Lord. We see the glory of God held up as of supreme importance for Jesus. We see Him conversing with God over the culminating events of His life that are about to transpire. And we see His concern for His people, that they might be one and that they might grow into the fullness of life in God.

Do we have the commitment to prayer that Jesus demonstrated? Without such a life of prayer, we will surely be on our own in seeking to change the world. But with it, nothing will be impossible for us (Matt. 21:22).

Jesus, then, is the Supreme World Changer. He provides for us a vision of the possibilities, of what might come to be if we labor faithfully to have the life of Jesus lived out in our own. Certainly we cannot expect that such an achievement will be realized overnight. We must be more realistic in our approach to following the vision that Christ sets forth for us.

Taking the Long View

Paul said that we would be changed into the image of Christ "from glory to glory" (2 Cor. 3:18). By this he meant that we should take a long view of our development as God's world changers. To become a people showing forth the glory of God is not something that "springs full-grown from the head of Zeus." We must set our course by the vision of Jesus Christ and determine that nothing will deter us from it. We must go forward one step at a time, following the leading of God's Spirit according to the teaching of His Word, seeking to bring the life of Christ into the whole of our lives more and more each and every day.

Like Jesus, we must learn to appreciate the value of contemplation, meditation, faith, circumspection, and obedience. We must allow the vision of Christ and the searching light of God's Word to bathe our whole lives with the beauty of God's holiness and of His perfect will. It will be hard work, requiring much attention, constant diligence, and a certain amount of failing. Yet, the alternative—a world that continues to fall ever further away from the love, truth, and goodness of God—is not something with which the believer can be content. Like Paul, we must determine to "follow after, if that I may apprehend that for which also I am apprehended of Christ Jesus" (Phil. 3:12). His advice is as sound today as ever: "Brethren, I count not myself to have apprehended; but this one thing I do, forgetting those things which are behind, and reaching forth unto those things which are before, *I press toward the mark for the prize of the high calling of God in Christ Jesus"* (Phil. 3:13-14, italics added). Oh, for such resolve among the people of God today!

Toward the end of His earthly ministry, there came to Jesus certain Greeks who said to one of His disciples, "Sir, we would see Jesus" (John 12:21). This is the attitude we need to cultivate. If we can set our minds, focus our hearts, and aim our very souls toward developing a new vision of Jesus for our lives, then from glory to glory we will begin to be like Him more and more. And, when that begins to happen, we will become that for which Christ has laid hold on us—that for which we have been created and recreated in Him—the world changers of this generation.

Questions for Study or Discussion

1. How did the writer of Hebrews describe the need to concentrate on the person of Christ? What is involved? What should we keep in mind? See Hebrews 12:1-3.

2. Which of the character traits of Jesus do you find most necessary for our day? Why?

For Further Reading

Thielicke, Helmut. *Between God and Satan.* Grand Rapids, Mich.: Wm. B. Eerdmans Publishing Co., 1973.
Stewart, James S. *The Life and Teaching of Jesus Christ.* Nashville, Tenn.: Abingdon.

ONE IN A MILLION
Derek Williams

The story of Billy Graham with Mission England

'There is no doubt that the three months during which I shared in Mission England were one of the highlights of my entire Ministry'. Billy Graham

Outlining the six regional missions in England during 1984, Derek Williams carefully links personal encounters with an interesting insight into what went on behind the scenes.

192 pages (including 16 pages of colour photographs)

ISBN 0-85009-054-7

£1.95

HE BEGAN WITH EVE
Joyce Landorf

Best-selling author Joyce Landorf's warm insight and wit beckon the modern world to learn from women of the Bible in this collection of fast moving character sketches. Using 'sanctified imagination', she puts herself into the sandals of these women as they confront all the trauma, emotions and excitement of life today.

ISBN 0-85009-058-X

£1.95

PRAYER: KEY TO REVIVAL
Paul Y Cho with R. Whitney Manzano

The secret behind the growth of the largest church in the world!

'No man can schedule a revival', Dr Cho has said, 'for God alone is the giver of life. But . . . when 'the fullness of time' is come and prayer ascends from a few earnest hearts, then history teaches it is time for the tide of revival to sweep in once more.'

This perspective is born of Dr Cho's conviction that while revival is the sovereign work of the Holy Spirit, the earnest prayers of God's people must work with the Spirit. It is then that He moves anew in the hearts of unbelievers.

ISBN 0-85009-059-8

£1.95

YOU CAN MAKE A DIFFERENCE
Tony Campolo

This book challenges young people to make their lives count for Christ. Tony Campolo uniquely identifies with young people in their own situation, then shows how they can use the power of God to change their world. With his incomparable blend of humour and serious biblical insights, the author deals with commitment, vocation, dating and discipleship.

ISBN 0-85009-056-3

£1.95

IT'S FRIDAY BUT SUNDAY'S COMIN'
Tony Campolo

'This book is Campolo at his best . . . in a world of mealie-mouthed compromise, it is long overdue and very welcome.'
Peter Meadows

This book is sensitive to the needs of both youth and adults for agape love, deeper than the cultural myth of romanticism . . . for acceptance and wholeness . . . for knowledge of God. It's bold claim is that while the world metes out its 'Fridays' of doom and gloom, the resurrection is the last work – 'Sunday's comin'!'

ISBN 0-85009-057-1

£1.60

EVIDENCE FOR JOY
Josh McDowell and Dale Bellis

Unlocking the secrets to love, acceptance and security

Reasons for faith are never a mere academic exercise for the authors. In this book they first show how Christian faith rests in a person, not a system; that it is intelligent, not blind; and that it is objective, rather than subjective. They then devote most of their work to a challenging discussion of how this kind of faith relates to our felt needs – for love, for acceptance and for security.

ISBN 0-85009-055-5

£1.95

THE DREAM
Keith Miller

In the Dream, Keith Miller invites us to go on an imaginative journey with him to try to look at ourselves and the church the way God might look at us.

It is not always a happy journey. In many ways, the story shows, we in God's church have let Him down – failing to love and forgive one another, by failing to reach outside ourselves and help those who are in need.

The book is pervaded with a sense of the Lord's sadness and righteous anger over these sins. But it also shines with His overwhelming love, concern and forgiveness. It is fundamentally, a book of hope.

ISBN 0-85009-061-X

£1.40

WORD LIFEWARE™

PRESENTING

TONY CAMPOLO ON VIDEO

YOU CAN MAKE A DIFFERENCE
A FOUR-PART SERIES FOR YOUTH

1 Commitment
Getting Beyond Good Intentions
"It is what we commit ourselves to that gives us identity, meaning and purpose in life, and commitment to Christ is the only commitment of lasting value."

2 Vocation
Setting the course and travelling light
"We have a responsibility to be in the places where we are most desperately needed ... do something great for Jesus. The time has come for a whole new generation."

3 Dating
Turning your love life over to Jesus
"Spirituality is caring for people who are hurting ... reach out to the kid who is left out and make him feel included — give Christian love."

4 Discipleship
Living life to the nth degree
"Study the Bible and get to know the Author. Set aside time to be inwardly still; to hear the voice of God. Get involved with a support group — you are empowered through fellowship. You need the Church and the Church desperately needs you."

YOU CAN MAKE A DIFFERENCE videos are just some of over 20 videos currently available from Word (UK).

Word Publishing
Word (UK) Ltd
Northbridge Road, Berkhamsted, Herts HP4 1EH

WORD LIFEWARE™

PRESENTING
TONY
CAMPOLO
ON VIDEO

IT'S FRIDAY, BUT SUNDAY'S COMIN'

"I'm not ashamed of the Gospel of Christ, because the Gospel of Christ meets every need of every human being on this planet."

IT'S FRIDAY, BUT SUNDAY'S COMIN' is a powerful message that has motivated Christian congregations around the country to seek a deeper, more costly commitment to Christ.

Dr Campolo's sharp, honest humour makes us laugh at our own short sightedness. His down to earth insight and persuasive arguments compel us to responsible action.

IT'S FRIDAY, BUT SUNDAY'S COMIN' videos are just some of over 20 videos currently available.

For further details of Word videos and other Word products please complete the coupon below.

Please send me information on:
Word Records/Cassettes ☐   Books   ☐
Lifelifter Cassettes   ☐   Video   ☐
(Please tick items of interest)

Name ....

Address ....

....

Word Publishing
Word (UK) Ltd
Northbridge Road, Berkhamsted, Herts HP4 1EH